GROW!

Seeds of Wisdom for Budding Leaders

BY
AMANDA URIBE

EST D *Made* 2013
SIMPLY
PURE

ISBN # 978-0-9969131-1-9
Published by Made Simply Pure, LLC.
Printed in the United States of America

Cover Art by Hannah Shields
www.beebuzzworthy.com

*This book is dedicated to my dad
for inspiring my love of writing and to my mom
for the gift of an adjective-filled life.
Thanks to the two of you, I am never without
the thoughts or the million ways to
tell the world about them.*

About the Author

Amanda Uribe joined Young Living in January 2013. In less than two years, she helped cultivate and grow hundreds of other budding leaders in her garden, reaching the rank of Diamond. She has been described as energetic, knowledgeable, and fun to be around – if only to watch what crazy adventure or situation she will get into next. She is passionate about her family – they are her greatest adventure! What makes this book even funnier to her husband is the fact that this leadership book is all about growing plants and gardens. As a Young Living metaphor, this succeeds greatly. In real life, his beautiful wife can't keep a plant alive for more than a week. Good thing she has Young Living – perhaps the only way plants thrive in the Uribe house.

Acknowledgements

My family is my life. I would be lost without my husband, Gabe, and the incredible ability he has to make me feel like I am the most amazing, beautiful wife and mother in the world – even on the days I feel more like Lucille Ball in some crazy mishap with cake all over my face. What makes it better is on those days, instead of shaking your head in exasperation, you smile and tell me at least I keep your life interesting. I love you, sweetheart. You changed my world forever the day you fell in love with me – which helped a ton since I was already head-over-heels for you. Here's to another twenty years together ... times several more lifetimes.

To my kids, Gage and Morgan, you totally changed my life in the best, most unbelievable way possible. What on earth did I do before I was a mom? I know I had more sleep. You are worth every minute of sleep deprivation. I love you to the moon and back forever. Hope this book shows you if mom can do it, you can do anything in the universe. Never be too scared to try. Aim for the moon. If you miss, at least you'll land among the stars. Love, Mommy.

To my parents and my sister, the early believers. All of you said I had a book in me somewhere. Thanks for believing I could do anything and everything. I'm not done yet. There is a whole lot of anything and everything out there still. Love you always and ever.

Lastly, I would like to thank each and every one of my team members in Young Living. None of this would be possible if you hadn't joined me on this adventure. Through laughter, tears, shared hopes and a few rough bumps in the road, you have been my anchor in life. You keep me grounded, laugh at my craziness, and to quote a great friend, "bless my socks off." Thank you all for joining me on this adventure. Love you.

Common Young Living Terms

Customer: Purchases Young Living at retail prices.

Member: Purchases Young Living at wholesale prices (24% off) – requires one purchase of 50pv in the calendar year to be active.

Sponsor: Direct upline and supporter of the newly enrolled member, receives 8% unilevel commission.

Enroller: Person who "enrolls" the new member in Young Living. Bonus commissions such as Fast Start are given to the enroller.

Rank: Your position within Young Living based on commissionable sales. Star, Senior Star, Executive, Silver, Gold, Platinum, Diamond, Crown Diamond, Royal Crown Diamond.

PV: Personal Volume: In essence, your purchase, though the total is the assigned personal volume points, not dollar amount. On essential oils, with a couple of exceptions, this point value is one for one, same with supplements. Diffusers, oil accessories, other Young Living products are less pv than their dollar amount.

PGV: Personal Group Volume – the pv in your personal team minus any existing business legs.

OGV: Overall Group Volume – the pv in your entire organization.

Essential Rewards: Young Living's monthly autoship program.

Start Living Bonus: $25 bonus for each enrollment of a member with a Premium Starter Kit or any 100pv Start Living Kit.

Fast Start Bonus: 25% commission on first three months pv of new enrollee, max of $200, 10% commission on first three months of those enrolled by new enrollee, max $80.

Legs: Branches of members directly underneath you, beginning with those members on level one.

Levels: Each level of members in your organization - essentially, the depth of your team.

Introduction

I magine, if you will, the time before the dawn of Walmart and Target or other major chain supercenters filled the horizon from east to west. In this era, the concept of shopping was far different than what we witness today. If you needed eggs, the neighbor had plenty from her coop for sale. Butter? Yep, got that, too! Jams, jellies, and pickled whatever. Peaches, apples, tomatoes, a whole garden for sale – pennies on the dollar. It was fresh, it was often organic, and it came locally from someone you knew and trusted. Goods outside of the garden were no different. Someone locally owned a sewing shop, a convenience store, a bakery, or a housewares shop. They knew you by name, asked about your family, and cared about your well-being. If you were sick, the whole town knew about it, and you could count on get-well staples being sent to your door from the local families. Well, times change – as they do – and the old was ushered out like leaves in fall, while new mega we-got-everything-you-can-imagine superstores took their place. Where Aunt Mae's bakery stood, now Publix stands. Where Sam had his convenience store and gas station, a Kroger advertising ten cents off the gallon now sits. On the street where a dozen businesses offered everything from home and garden to lawn and auto, the retail giant Walmart plopped itself down and built a supercenter over the heart of town. Now, no one knows your name. No one is glad you came. Personal relationships are a thing of the distant past. We get out of the car, dash into the store, grab a bunch of overpriced items sent from China and grown God-Knows-Where, while talking on our cell phones and leaving as fast as we came. To remind us just how impersonal life has become, we now have self-checkout counters. Literally, you can walk in the store, get what you need, checkout and get into your car, never having spoken a single word to anyone. Yet, we wonder why the world has become so unfriendly, so narcissistic, so eager to cast stones. Really? Isn't it obvious?

The relationships we were a part of used to define who we were. Now, we are defined by how much money we make, what kind of car we drive, and the size of our home. What happened to the relationships? Cast off to the wayside along with all of the businesses of yesteryear. We not only lost a small piece of Americana, we lost a piece of our humanity – *our connectivity*. Looking at todays and tomorrows with an ever-widening gap of our past and future, how can we encourage and foster the relationships we all need?

Thankfully, one last venue of market-based friendship still exists today. The Multi-level Market (Our one remaining "mom and pop" shop: providing face-to-face commerce built upon a relationship), a business grown out of common needs and quality products provided. A home-based business giving moms and dads everywhere the opportunity to go back to the basics and build without the pressure of competing with grand storefronts of major corporations. These businesses thrive because of the personal relationship built with customers who know you offer a great product, the knowledge to teach and share about it, and the desire to help them be happy and healthy. Without the relationship, these businesses are nothing. It is what sets them apart from the crowd. It is what makes them desirable to both business builder and consumer. In addition to relationship building, the degree of your success correlates directly to your investment in education, acquisition of resources, time management, and your willingness to lead from the front. Multi-level Marketing. Network Marketing. Relationship Marketing. Regardless of the term used, what most people hearing these terms focus on is the word MARKETING. Selling something. There is a certain stigma attached with the term marketing. Why? We market and are marketed to every single day. Some of these are truly necessary items, others perhaps not so much. What makes one person's ideas or products more marketable than another's? Simply put, it is connectivity. A certain connection the buyer feels with the marketer or product. In some instances, the product may be inferior, not needed, and a waste of money. So, why then was it purchased? The marketer. He/she made a connection. Commonality of thought and purpose were found. A relationship was established. This relationship, once forged, was powerful enough to entice someone to try the product.

In Network Marketing, this concept is the basis for which every organization either succeeds or fails. Successful leaders will recognize the opportunity and seize the moment. What are they seeing that you don't see? The opportunity for friendship, for a long lasting relationship based on a common interest. Okay, so what exactly is the interest then? The product. Really, it is truly that simple. If you believe in your product, – its value and need – and believe the more people you can help by introducing them to it, the better their world will be, then you have all the elements needed to begin a great relationship.

Is a relationship REALLY that important? Yes, yes, yes – a thousand times yes! Think about the relationships you currently have in your life. Parents, siblings, spouse, friends, children. When you call to mind one of these people, how do you feel? If you have a great relationship with them, you probably just smiled. This person has been in all of your great memories and adventures. They have shared in your successes, cheering you on with the loudest voice in the crowd. They were there to pick you up off the floor when you fell flat on your face with failure. Your relationship with them is one of the key aspects of what has made you who you are today.

Okay, so now imagine this new friend. You want them to try out Young Living essential oils. On day one, you meet them, hand them a business card, and ask them if they want to become a member and purchase a Premium Starter Kit. You know it is such an amazing value, and the company one of the best on the planet. Of course they want to become a member; who wouldn't? Well, to start with, the new friend you almost had a budding relationship with until you tried to market them a product before really getting to know them.

How then, do you help others learn about essential oils and begin their Young Living adventure? Simple. Begin a relationship. Everything centers around your relationships. Think about it for a moment. As you go about your average day, you weave yourself in and out of one relationship to the next. In each instance, you are either imparting information or receiving it – sometimes both. These relationships either grow and flourish or wither and die based on your efforts. At this point in your life's journey, you can probably think of one or two friends in whom you invested time, attention, and love. Keeping the relationship strong means you contact them regularly, celebrate successes with them, and lend a shoulder or ear during the tough times. These actions firmly cement your friendship. They build memories whereby each of you can call to mind dozens of times you were there for one another. Conversely, you can probably recall a few foundling friendships, which you intended to nurture and see blossom into a lifelong relationship, only to have busy schedules and life issues cause you to lose sight of one another and fall out of friendship. Sure, you think about one another time and again, but it never develops into picking up the phone or getting together. If this is sounding all too familiar, rest assured, you are not alone. All of us are guilty of great intentions swallowed by daily commitments. How can we change this? Why does it even matter? Think of relationships like a garden. Water them and provide them with care and nutrients; they will thrive. Ignore them, or be sporadic in their care or your time spent in the garden, they will surely perish.

When looking at an MLM versus a storefront business, the major difference is in the relationship. Think back in history before we had massive storefronts. Pioneer life centered around bartering, selling, and exchanging with friends. One woman made preserves and home baked goods and would sell them to her friends and neighbors, while another sold her eggs, and yet another sold fruits and vegetables from her garden. Their friends and neighbors purchased these goods for two reasons: they were helping out a friend and they knew their friend was supplying them with great quality items at a good value. This practice still continues today in the MLM industry. This business has allowed us to operate without the massive (involved with a storefront, and brought us back to the basi our love of a product with our friends, and build a residual income from our networking – all the while selling a commodity we value and trust for our own families.

Can it really be that simple? Yes. Young Living's sharing slogan captures it best. "Love it. Share it." It doesn't get much easier than that. So let's talk about how to accomplish this and grow a garden of Young Living members as in love with their products as you are with yours.

Before anything else can be done, you must find your "why".Why are you doing this? Is it only for wealth? To purchase products you love with earned commission? Perhaps it is something deeper. Many members start out with the sole goal of getting their products paid for with earnings. There is nothing wrong with this goal. More often than not, though, you fall in love with the company, the farms, the products, the philanthropy – the mission of Young Living. Know the mission statement of this company:

"We honor our stewardship to champion nature's living energy, essential oils, by fostering a community of healing and discovery while inspiring individuals to wellness, purpose, and abundance."

Think about that for a minute. So simple, yet so complex. A company, which values nature, what nature gives us, what we return to nature by recycling, and the hidden beauty within the plants most overlooked. A company, which fosters a spirit of health and wellness – of mind, body, and spirit – through use of God's beautiful creation. A company, which aspires to teach and provide health and financial wellness, purpose, and abundance to all who join. It is easy to see why so many people have fallen head over heels for this company for decades. With a corresponding vision statement: *to bring Young Living to every home in the world.* This company is the personification of generosity and love. After you have gone on recognition trips to some of the farms and the school, met the families in Croatia,

Uganda, Ecuador or other locations where the Young Living Foundation provides food, clothing, shelters, schooling, and other necessities, you will fully understand there just aren't any other companies of Young Living's caliber. Its founder, Gary Young, has devoted every waking minute of his life in the pursuit of this vision and mission. Whether you become passionate about Young Living's vision and works of philanthropy, or you develop your own "why," you *must* have a purpose.

1

Starting a Garden

To plant a garden is to believe in tomorrow.
- Audrey Hepburn

L ife in a garden . . . serene . . . beautiful . . . the perfect oasis. There is a reason King Louis XIV built all the expansive gardens in and around Versailles. Renowned for their beauty, they are quite simply a masterpiece. Several centuries later, people still tour these gardens, struck with a sense of awe and amazement at the vision and the sheer amount of work it took to create such a marvelous estate. A garden can be so many things. It can be a refuge, a sanctuary of Mother Nature, and a peaceful spot to rest. It can be a veritable bounty of edible blessings to provide us with a nutritious harvest. It can sustain and nourish the human soul and body like nothing else. Conversely, it can be a chore. A task never-ending. Morning, noon, night, the garden calls for attention. Weather, soil, bugs, and the most ugly of weeds all seek to take residence in the garden. They require constant management and care. Without a committed gardener, the garden will perish to the unsavory elements.

Much like the garden, your business can be a masterpiece of your enterprise or it can become a ramshackle collection of overgrown weeds and bugs feasting on the remains of your lackluster attempt at growing. To be a success in business doesn't happen overnight. It is a path filled with hard labor and countless hours of effort. Some of your undertakings will be successful and others will explode like a hurled rotten tomato, ruining your best shirt along with your spirit. Success is not measured by one monumental task, rather it is the summation of hundreds of smaller tasks performed again and again, day after day, week after week, until you reach the pinnacle of completion. Only after these countless efforts can we imagine, sit, and enjoy the garden – our own private Versailles. When beginning your business, ask yourself, "What is the goal here? Am I building Versailles, or am I happy with a container garden?" The difference .. . Versailles will yield a dividend for life and the container garden will provide a few meals . . . nothing more.

As with any garden, a great deal of preparation must be made – one does not just grab a seedling and stick it in the dirt, expecting it to grow and flourish. Well, some might, but seriously, does this ever really work? First, the area needs to be prepared. Fertile soil is where plants grow best. In your Young Living garden, this is going to be you. Educate yourself about the products. What is the history of Young Living? What products do they have and which farms do they come from? What do they do? Which body systems do they help support? Research, research, research. Read everything you can find on essential oils. It is readily available on the Internet and in reference materials. Attend classes in your area. These are often hosted by Young Living corporate as well as amazing leaders across the globe. In learning everything about Young Living and their products, you are setting yourself up for success. Not only will you be able to answer questions, you will feel so much more confident with this knowledge. KNOWLEDGE IS POWER. Knowledge of essential oils can make the difference between your members going on to learn, use, and love essential oils or floundering with a box of pretty oils they end up sticking in a cabinet after months of failed attempts to use them. No one expects you to know all the answers, but they do expect you to know where to find them quickly and efficiently. Passing on knowledge to your members – training them on the wellness aspects of their product – not only enhances their knowledge and contributes to their personal enjoyment with the oils but also determines, to a large part, whether they succeed or fail at the business.

Now that you have fertile soil, what's next? Start looking for the perfect seedlings to establish your garden! As with any great garden, you will encounter variety and differences in the people you meet. You will need to understand the differences in your seedlings from the start so you can adequately support them and their needs. Just like all plants cannot be treated the same, neither can people. Water English ivy too much and it will still flourish; water a cactus too much and it will surely die. People are much the same. Some love you lavishing time and attention on them, and want that personal touch. They light up when they have your focused efforts and friendship. To them, a personal touch means you truly care about their health and happiness. Others would prefer a more business-like relationship. They want concise, clear information. They like you, but they aren't interested in developing a personal relationship. Figuring out the personalities you are working with is key. Are they outgoing or introverted? Calm or energetic? Quiet or loud? There is nothing worse to quiet, shy, introverted people than when they are faced with a larger-than-life personality forcing them to go outside of their comfort zones. These details matter, so spend some serious time figuring all this out.

2

The Hesitant Seedling

Don't judge each day by the harvest you reap,
but by the seeds you plant.
- Robert Louis Stevenson

Some people take awhile to get accustomed to new ideas. They hesitantly test the environment around them before committing to the adventure. As potential new members of Young Living, they will need you to foster a relationship encouraging them to ask questions and explore the world of essential oils. Invite them to both live and online classes. Often, hesitant, somewhat shy people are more at ease attending classes online from the comfort of their own home. Having multiple venues for them to get the information will be key. Something as simple as meeting them for coffee can be so beneficial in getting them to share questions, stories, or ideas. The quiet ones are powerful. They seldom join in the conversation, but when they do, everyone listens to hear what they will say, for surely it must be something interesting and worthwhile to get them to jump into the conversation. In leadership, the hesitant seedling will benefit greatly from one-on-one learning opportunities and guidance. Remember, your goal is not to shape the seedling into your ideal of a great leader. They need to find their own path of growth and leadership. This will look different to everyone. You are simply the guide. Be sure to offer suggestions and help with business; mentor them, but do not take the leadership role away from them. Often, the quiet people get ran over by the more gregarious people in life. Take the time to listen so you will understand how to guide without squashing out the personality of your teammate.

3

The Outgoing Seedling

Gardens are not made by singing "Oh How Beautiful"
and sitting in the shade.

Others you come across are quite outgoing. They have no problem telling you exactly what they think, need, or question. Often, these seedlings will be the self-starters. They easily embrace the opportunity to teach, share, and help others learn about essential oils. Helping them find their path may seem so easy many leaders will step back and allow the seedling to forge ahead on their own. This may or may not work well. On one hand, someone who is confident, outgoing, and self-motivated may be a great member in Young Living, learning all about the oils and supplements, along with the history and research behind them. They will probably immerse themselves in Young Living and quickly become a great resource to those around them. In leadership, they will be an enthusiastic and dynamic leader able to connect and effortlessly build relationships with their team. On the other hand, the outgoing, dynamic leader may be so accustomed to forging the path, they may fail to ask for help when needed, or may be overlooked by their leadership simply because they seem to have figured out everything. Just as in a garden, if the plants looked watered, the gardener may have his or her attention elsewhere. Skipping out on time with this leader may result in missed adventure, learning, and growth! Be on the lookout for opportunities to mentor this leader in areas they may overlook or falter – they may seem to have it all together, but few of us actually ever do.

4

Colorful Blossoms

The seeds of acceptance sprout quickly,
plant one today and see what bursts forth.

All of us, regardless of which category seedling we fall into, have unique personalities. Much like the blossoms in a garden, some will be showy and vibrant, others delicate and fair. If we are to have a thriving garden, we have to learn the language of the flowers. What does this mean exactly? Imagine trying to speak English to a German speaker. How effective is it? Not very. The same holds true with our basic forms of communication. Based on our personalities, we may communicate with very short, succinct sentences, or with long, colorful, adjective-filled sentences. Our stories may be full of details and take an hour in the telling, or be to the point in five minutes or less. We may enjoy our surroundings to be filled with noise and raucous laughter or quiet with serenity and peaceful sounds. The key to communicating across a broad spectrum of personalities is to speak the language of your audience. To do this, first you must know your own personality. Second, figure out the personality of the person you are engaging in conversation. Only then will we be able to share our minds and hearts, knowing the other person is fully engaged and listening. There are numerous personality tests online. One of my favorites is the shape test.[1] This test has been around since the early 1990's and is widely used in businesses still today to illuminate the differences in our personalities and show how we can use this knowledge to our advantage. Let's have some fun for a moment or two and take the quiz!

First, imagine if you will, a series of shapes as follows: square, triangle, circle, and squiggle. Eyes closed. Come on, play along. Really imagine. Which one are you drawn to first? The beautiful sharp, crisp edges of the square? The elegant sweeping arch of the triangle? The curvy beauty of the circle? Perhaps the lovely squiggly lines? Have you narrowed in on one? Okay. The results are in:

If you picked a square you are more than likely:

Routine oriented; organized and structured

Task oriented; very hard worker

Loyal

Think logically and methodically

Analytical; value the details and data

Know and follow the policies and rules

Prefer working alone to working in a team

Conservative

Need more information and research – never enough

Calendar driven; orderly and scheduled

Possibly stubborn

Sometimes see fun as a luxury

---

1   Dellinger, S. (1989). Psycho-geometrics: How to use geometric psychology to influence people. Prentice Hall Direct.

Meeting arrival: "A full fifteen minutes early and I am on time. I wonder when everyone else is going to get here? Where are they?"

Meeting behavior: show up with a ton of notes, extremely prepared, and get right down to work.

Motto: "Give me a goal and a deadline – it will be done ahead of schedule and flawlessly."

Ways to improve on your perfection:

Be more tolerant with others

Allow yourself some mistakes

Take a break from the structured routine

Learn to make decisions without all the details.

Be spontaneous every once in a while.

If you picked triangle, you are more than likely:

Competitive

Confident

Outspoken; love to debate

No nonsense

Need to know WHY

Focused on goals

Driven to succeed and motivated by results

Like to take charge and move fast

See the big picture – no need for research or details

Decisive – cut to the chase and move on!

Impatient

Meeting arrival: 5 minutes early and you are on time!

Meeting behavior: "Seriously? We have to have a meeting? Just give me the bottom line and carry on!"

Motto: "Okay, copy that, what's next??"

Ways to improve upon your perfection:

Pay closer attention to the smaller details

Be aware of the impact you have on others

Give people time to come around to your ideas

Slow down and take interest in more of the details

If you picked a circle, you are more than likely:

A people person

Fun-loving and social

Love to hear the whole story and tell yours

Listen and communicate well

Like to have teams, groups, committees

Avoid conflict or unpopular decisions

Often over commit; people pleaser

Are better at caring for others than yourself

Don't care for status symbols and hierarchy

Have great empathy and concern for everyone

Meeting Arrival: "eh, 5 minutes late and I'm still practically on time!

Meeting Behavior: "Let's talk about our lives for a bit first and chat about the universe, then get down to business."

Motto: "You want me to do that for you? Sure, I can make time!"

Ways to improve upon your perfection:

Learn to be timely and straight to the point when necessary

Worry less about what other people think and do.

Learn how to say no and stick to it

Hold yourself and others accountable

Seize an opportunity to take charge and develop your ideas

If you picked squiggle, you are most likely:

A visionary; full of great ideas and concepts

Creative

Have a ton of energy and enthusiasm

Like to try new and different things

Have a problem finishing tasks you start

Lack structure and organization

Easily bored without new stimulus

Think and act fast on your ideas; can appear flakey

Don't wear a watch

Meeting arrival: "Well, I intended to get there on time, but got side-tracked on the way there and stopped a few times. At least I made it before you gave up on me and went home!"

Meeting Behavior: "Let's grab a quick bite to eat and discuss what's new first. Then we can move on to business – I have tons of ideas!"

Motto: "Absolutely! I can do that! Can we spice it up a little bit? Don't worry, I can squeeze it in my schedule!

Ways to improve upon your perfection:

Slow down and think about actions.

Be intentional in thoughts and actions.

Wear a watch and practice keeping time during your day.

Begin task-oriented organization by keeping a note book/calendar.

Work on having commitment after the feeling of excitement is long gone.

You've probably been able to identify yourself in one of these shapes. Most people have a dominant shape and traces of others. Identifying yourself is step one. Figuring out how to capitalize on your strengths and tackle your weaknesses is key. Do yourself a favor and write down those things you excel at first so you can see in black and white how blessed you are to be you! Next, write down those traits you may wish to cultivate a bit. Let's be clear: you are who you are, and you are ". . . fearfully and wonderfully made." – Psalm 139:14 – DO NOT CHANGE WHO YOU ARE. The goal here is not a metamorphosis from caterpillar to butterfly, but rather finding out how you can be your best "you" using both your rock star qualities *and* those you deem not quite up to snuff. Only when we know and fully appreciate ourselves, can we begin to know and fully appreciate others.

Now that you know who you are, you need to figure out whom you are meeting with and learn to speak their language. An example of this is Margaret. She is definitely a square. She has all the details worked out, including the tiniest ones most would overlook. She travels with her planner and notebook because she never knows when she needs to fill those pages! Today, Margaret is her usual 15 minutes early for a meeting with Emma. No nonsense, she is prepared with facts, graphs, history, and research on essential oils. She knows Young Living is an amazing company and is certain once Emma hears all about it, she will sign up immediately. While waiting for Emma, who seems to be running behind today, she begins planning future meetings and jotting down goals. The meeting time comes and goes with no sign of Emma. Margaret, who has been glancing at her watch every few minutes, getting slightly more annoyed with every glance, is exasperated Emma could not make it on time. About 15 minutes later, just as Margaret is ready to pack up and head home, Emma breezes in with a carefree, happy spirit and plops down next to Margaret. She is talking about her morning, laughing about something that happened, asking if Margaret is doing well. On the outside, Margaret looks happy. Nothing could be further from the truth at this point. She is angry. Irritated at Emma for being late, for being so carefree and for appearing lackadaisical while Margaret, herself, has spent so much time being the very model of preparedness and business.

The meeting does not go well. Emma continues to be spontaneous and totally distracted, jumping up to get a slice of cheesecake while interjecting stories to Margaret's presentation whenever something triggers a memory. Bumping her chair back into the table behind them, she engages the woman there in a ten-minute conversation. Emma then senses Margaret is getting slightly annoyed, though she can't pinpoint why, and after a few minutes – deciding Margaret must have other things to do and perhaps the meeting went too long – is off to her next adventure. Margaret is left feeling frustrated and angry, while Emma is confused and a bit overwhelmed by all of the information Margaret presented. What happened? Nothing bad. They were simply speaking different languages. If Margaret had evaluated Emma's personality before the meeting, she would have known how to adjust her presentation – and her expectations – to meet Emma's needs and enjoy the meeting herself. Why isn't it up to Emma to adjust her personality traits? Well, to start with, Emma is coming to a meeting requested by Margaret. Emma is just there for friendship and fun – maybe a great slice of cheesecake. As the one seeking out Emma to join Young Living, Margaret needs to be the one to adjust her personality and expectations. Make sense? If Margaret knew what her own hot button issues were and knew Emma's personality type, she could have gone into the meeting with the expectation that Emma may not enjoy tons of details, Powerpoints, research, and graphics. Emma would probably enjoy a narrative approach best. Margaret would have expected Emma to be a bit late and adjusted her thinking to being there her usual 15 minutes early with the intent to sit back and enjoy the solitude until Emma arrived. She would have been prepared to chat about life, family, the weather, and the latest adventure Emma had this morning. Being more relaxed with this in mind, Margaret would have enjoyed sharing the oily stories of her life versus the research behind her oily life. Most likely, Emma would have had a fabulous time with Margaret, and when she bumped into the lady behind their table, the conversation would have been a threesome with Young Living adventures as the focal point. Who knows? She could have gotten them both to sign up with Young Living! This story clearly illustrates why it is important to know what type of "shape" your friend is, and communicate with them in a way based on their personality. In the end, you will find greater success – and a better flow – to both your business and personal relationships. It is far easier to embrace and celebrate each other's differences than to continually measure oneself against the ruler of another. Learning to come together and meld our personalities, even for a brief time, allows everyone to just sit back and enjoy the adventure together.

5

Friendship Before Oils

A single rose can be my garden...
a single friend, my world.
- Leo Buscaglia

With all this in mind, you may be ready to launch a full-scale oily revolution at all of your neighbors, friends, and loved ones. In order to achieve success, you must realize a couple of things. First, this new adventure into essential oils may be exciting and fun for you, but it may be foreign and scary to someone who isn't familiar with these products. Go SLOW. Second, if all of the sudden, your entire friendship revolves around essential oils, your friends may take a giant step back. They aren't used to this healthy obsession you have just yet. Ease into it like you are stretching for a marathon. For, in fact, it IS a marathon. You are not in Young Living to do the 100-meter oil dash and sign up whomever you can. You are in this for life and are growing a relationship with Young Living. Your goal is to show your friends and loved ones the health and happiness you have as part of this company. Seeing it, they will naturally want to share it with you sooner or later. The goal then becomes to guide them, educate them, love them, and show them how they, too, can have a relationship with Young Living. The marathon, like any other, is an adventure based on one's ability to "go the distance." For you, this means a varied exercise program of sharing, caring, and educating long-term. When someone signs up, you are NOT DONE. You must empower them to continue learning about health and wellness. If you fail, they will not realize the value in Young Living and discontinue their membership. All of your hard work in getting them to join will have been for naught.

6

The Rule of Thirds

Friendship is always a sweet responsibility,
never an opportunity.
- Khalil Gibran

good rule of thumb is the rule of thirds. Just like in photography using the rule of thirds to balance a photo's scene, remember to have balance in your oily sharing. For every conversation in which you discuss Young Living, be sure the next two have nothing to do with essential oils and everything to do with conversations that build your relationship. One third Young Living, two-thirds relationship fun. A relationship where one friend only discusses Young Living 24/7 and the other friend tries to share life and memories will be too one-sided and narrow to stand the test of time. Build the relationship based on common interests, shared adventures, and conversations, which strengthen your bond as friends. Interjecting Young Living one in three conversations is probably sufficient and won't seem obnoxious to a friend who knows you have a new passion. In a new friendship, this is extremely important and cannot be stressed enough. You do not want to be that friend who goes on incessantly about Young Living and has nothing more to offer in the way of friendship. Despite the phenomenal nature of this company, there is only so much one can hear on the same topic without crying uncle. Having this rule firmly cemented in your mind will enable you to realize when you have over-shared and how much effort you should be making to create a bond of friendship based on a full-spectrum of life's adventures.

7

When Teaching

You must plant many seeds to get a good harvest.

To educate your members effectively, be sure you are hosting classes at a minimum once every ten days. If scheduling permits, once a week. These classes should be diverse, covering not only essential oils and supplements, but also health and wellness. Keep classes simple, easy to duplicate, and respectful of everyone's time. A two or three-hour class will not only find you exhausted, it will find you lacking in participants – not many people have the desire to sit in a long class. About an hour to an hour and a half is perfect. It gives you enough time to cover the basics and touch on the key focus of your class, as well as give time for questions at the end.

The way you teach should be indicative of your personality and style. It is, after all, your class. Just be sure you are, once again, going back to the principal of shapes. Having too much research and data means you probably lost the attention of the circles and squiggles within the first 15 minutes. Having too much fluff means you probably lost the squares and triangles in the first 15 minutes as well. When developing your class, try to keep participants in mind and add a bit of diversity to your slides or information to keep everyone engaged. There is an old saying, "facts tell and stories sell." Keep this in mind when presenting slides, information, or data to your class.

Most people can easily call to mind the details when sharing a story. When given a series of data-based facts and figures, it is much more difficult to call to mind.

An example of this is the story of Maria. She takes Young Living Multigreens and Ningxia Red everyday and loves them. When teaching, she lists the ingredients on the bottle and tells the class they should all be taking Multigreens. The class may or may not see the need for this product. Do they know the ingredients and their health value? Probably not. In the next class, Maria tells a story about Multigreens. She explains some of the key ingredients and talks about not getting enough vegetables and nutrients in her daily diet. She tells them about a woman who gets up early, runs around all day like a high-speed sports car, and by lunch she is lagging behind in the race. Usually too busy to stop and eat, she grabs whatever is handy – a candy bar and an apple – and keeps on running. By two in the afternoon, she is like a car on empty. Mentally and physically, she is exhausted. Her body is just not getting what it needs to maintain and function at optimal levels. By the time she gets home to her sweet family, she has nothing left to give. She puts a quick ready-made dinner for everyone on the table and preps for the next day. After the kids go to bed, she does a quick cleaning or maybe a load of laundry. Maria then tells them this woman was her life before Young Living. She tells them how she drinks Ningxia Red to boost her energy and support her busy body's needs. She tells them she has noticed the biggest difference in her mental stamina and ability to perform at work with the addition of Young Living's supplements. Maria has masterfully illustrated for the class why they, too, need Young Living supplements. Hearing these stories along with the research and facts about these products will provide the class with a well-rounded education on Young Living, their products, and why no home should ever be without them. The stories Maria interjects in her presentation will keep her audience engaged, and help them remember what she was presenting long after the class has ended.

Education is a powerful tool. Your Young Living business depends on you teaching in a way that will inspire your members to try new products. Let's say for example, you offer a special incentive for your downline if they order Mineral Essence. Not knowing what it is, no one takes you up on this offer. Think about it. Would you purchase more to get something you value at nothing? Probably not. However, let's assume you teach on the benefits of Mineral Essence. You tell them there are 62 trace minerals in this product. They are in ionic form, which is the most optimal way to get them for utilization by the body. You discuss how over-farming, and polluted oceans have depleted the minerals from the dirt and contaminated the ones we eat from seafood. You speak about how today's nutritional content in the foods we eat is not the same as that of our ancestors hundreds of years ago – we don't eat wholesome nutrient-rich foods, we eat food substitutes. Where nutrients and minerals used to exist, now chemicals and by-products flourish. Learning about body systems, the support they need to function properly, and the lack of readily available minerals in our food supply, we quickly realize we must use supplements for our health. Now, let's go back to the special incentive. You offer a bottle of Mineral Essence for free to anyone placing a 200pv order. Two things will happen. One, you were smart enough to offer a special above the 190pv mark Young Living offers their monthly member special so those ordering will get both your incentive and Young Living's free product and, two because you did such a spectacular job educating on the necessity of minerals for great health, everyone will want to try it! Education cannot be stressed enough. Educate, educate, educate. Just as in life, knowledge is powerful. Sharing it can make your business. Withholding it can break your business.

This concept goes for your budding leaders as well. You must educate and do so fully. A leader lacking in education will be lacking in growth. A leader lacking in education will depend on you entirely, making you a prisoner of your own failure to educate. You need your budding leaders to be educated and confident for not only their success, but yours! Remember though, there is a difference between educating and supporting. Once you have educated your leaders, they will run with this knowledge, but your job is not done. Support never stops.

8

Business Education

The flower doesn't dream of the bee.
It blossoms and then the bee comes.
- Mark Nepo

The same holds true of educating on the business of Young Living. Do you remember the last time you thought about jumping feet first into a brand new business you knew nothing about, with no guaranteed income, little support or education, and no team to help you develop a plan of action for success? Ummmm. You said no. Really? Who wouldn't want that spectacular opportunity to struggle and fall flat on their face in failure? Surely, the wheels are turning in your head right now. Members without education on the business, support in their efforts, and a team of people beside them ready to offer wisdom and encouragement will not view a Young Living business as a worthwhile opportunity. Understandably, you may hesitate in sharing about the business side of things in an effort not to sound like a pushy car salesman, but if you fail to share at all, you risk suppressing a budding business leader by neglecting to offer them the same business education you received and saw value in attempting for your family.

To do this without sounding like you are all about business – which you are not; you are all about health and healthy business. It just makes sense! – remember to share those ideas that first got you excited about Young Living. You can stay at home with your kids. You can set your own hours. You can work with like-minded people. You can share a product you believe in, inspiring people to greater health and wellness. The list goes on and on. There are too many great reasons to do this as a business to list them all. By reviewing the benefits, you have determined you would be doing them a giant disservice by not sharing the business side of things with them. So share. Share like a friend. Share like you share that amazing crockpot recipe. Share like you share an opportunity you couldn't pass up. Share like you can't possibly keep such a blessing in your life secret. *Because it is all of those things.* Friends share opportunity, passion, and adventure. A Young Living business is *all* of those things and so much more.

9

Grow with Nutrients

Anyone can count the seeds in an apple.
No one can count the apples in a seed.

In order to grow effectively as a member and business in Young Living, you will need to be a product of the product. If you have never heard this statement before, what it means is you must use the product. Not only use the product, but BE the product. Use it, share it, live it! How can you effectively talk about a product's health benefits if you have not tried it yourself? You must know how it looks, tastes, makes you feel, and how it is beyond valuable for your own health and wellness before you can convince anyone else of its value. Obviously, on day one, you have a limited stock of essential oils and supplements, so you will be discussing products you have never tried yourself. It is unavoidable, but you can and should spend a great deal of time learning about them nonetheless. Over time, as your supply of Young Living products grows, you will be able to fully explore and appreciate them firsthand. Don't wait to share or teach until you have done this, though, or you may be waiting years to begin sharing. Start sharing and teaching immediately, and let your Young Living pantry grow while doing so!

Most families in Young Living surround themselves with Young

Living products everyday. The average Young Living family has our company's toothpastes, shampoos and conditioners, and beauty products in their bathrooms. They have a pantry stocked with dozens of vitamins and supplements taken daily for optimal health. They diffuse, wear, and ingest essential oils several times a day for a multitude of reasons. You will find out soon enough you depend on your Young Living products to stay healthy and happy, and using them daily will ensure you truly know your products inside and out!

10

Essential Rewards – truly ESSENTIAL

My garden is my favorite teacher.
- *Betsy Cañas Garmon*

The very best way to experience all of the products Young Living has to offer is by putting yourself on Essential Rewards. It is an optional program where the member agrees to purchase a minimum of 50pv in products every month on an autoship plan. This plan is flexible. Oils can be changed in and out each month. Processing dates can be changed as needed. Even a grace month can be used once in the year if you are not expecting commission. In exchange for this special program commitment, they will get back 10% of their purchase in essential rewards points to be used later to get FREE products. After month six in the program, 15% back, and after the twelfth month, a whopping 20% back in oil points! Not only this, but they will get reduced shipping for their essential rewards purchase. A couple details to note: you can begin using your free points after the third month, most essential oils and supplements have full point value (pv), but other products (such as diffusers, cases, non-oily supplies) will have less than full value. Lastly, you can discontinue the essential rewards program with a simple phone call at anytime, but you seriously won't want to quit! Honestly, for a member who loves Young Living's products and essential oils,

Essential Rewards is ... well ... essential.

Another great way to learn about Young Living in the months it will take you to have everything you dream of, is to pick three oils or supplements a week and learn everything you can about them. Google them, research them; really delve into the literature and websites devoted to teaching about them. Take notes – lots and lots of notes! By taking a few a week, you will find it very manageable to learn and share, and before you know it, you will have covered them all. Remember the childhood riddle, "How do you eat an elephant?" – the answer was so simple: "one bite at a time." You don't need to swallow the information at one time, small bites will do! Be sure you are taking the information and notes you have and sharing them! Only in sharing can we cement the knowledge we have gained. Make it a point to share with three people and you will most certainly retain the information forevermore.

While learning about the products, you would be wise to start a health journal. Any notebook will do. Just grab a pen and start writing. Things to write about: new product you tried, how it tasted, smelled, felt on skin. After a week of using it, how do you personally feel – both mentally and physically? Don't just write about the products. Give yourself a full health evaluation. What are you eating? Are you sleeping enough at night? Any major aches or issues? In journaling your experience, you will be able to see for yourself exactly how these products are affecting your health and well-being.

11

Nurture the Seeds

All the flowers of tomorrow are in the seeds of today.
- Indian Proverb

B y now you are probably trying to wrap your mind around how to learn all you can about Young Living and go out and teach the masses. There are several ways to do this, and one way is not better than any other. The way you teach will be a mix of your personality, style of teaching, and available time to do so. Remember, if you enjoy teaching, it will show. If you dread it, this will show as well. Put your heart and mind into the effort. What's the old saying: "Anything worth doing is worth doing well." Give it your best shot; you've nothing to lose. Be sure to really know the company and what sets us apart from everyone else. If you are passionate about why you only use Young Living for your family's health and wellness, people will listen. Passionate people are infectious. Know what type of classes you will teach. Let's explore the different style of classes currently being held all over the world by Young Living members.

First, informal classes. This style of class is laid back, often in a comfortable location such as a home, coffee shop, or park. No slideshows on giant screens here. Class will be an adventure in sharing. The instructor typically leads a group discussion, sharing stories, product tips and ideas, and encourages group participation. Hosted more like a social event, this class is an easy way to teach without being the center of everyone's attention. Think of it more as a social gathering with a bit of oily education.

Second, the online class. This style of class is a more modern approach to teaching. If you have ever taken an online class before, you know the information is presented and you can choose to view it or not. One format of online teaching, the "webinar," allows class members to see and hear an instructor video. Sometimes, the view is just of the person speaking. Other times, there is a slideshow or infographics shown on the screen. As a student, you can often rewind, forward, repeat, and pause to meet your needs. Quite often, the link for the presentation can be shared with all of your friends so more people can learn with you! A second format of online teaching is the "social media class." Most often, this is on Facebook. The instructor will create an event day and time and invite all class members. It is not uncommon for classmates to be able to invite all of their friends, as well. At the start of the class, the instructor will typically post an introductory photo and post. After the launch of this post, many more will follow. Typical classes will have twenty to thirty numbered posts with graphics and information. It is necessary to number the posts as, depending on comments, the post may rise to the top or be buried at the bottom of the class. Numbering enables members to search posts in order. Many times, these posts will include links to further information or videos for the students to watch. A social media class can have all postings loaded continuously for an hour, or throughout a day or two. The class is typically left up for a few days so all students are able to access the material according to the dictates of their schedule.

Third, the more formal class. This style of class is like the kind you remember from high school or college. Students sitting at tables, information and products around the room, perhaps a Powerpoint presentation on a screen behind you. You are standing in front of a group of students furiously taking notes on your presentation and, aside from a few brief moments of questions, all eyes are on you for the duration of the class. This style of class works best for the extrovert, but that does not mean it cannot be taught by anyone with a desire to teach this way.

Fourth, the Make and Take. This style of class is messy, but a fun kind of messy. Everyone comes with the expectation of learning while having a bit of fun. Typically, the instructor has chosen 6-12 different recipes for students to learn, while making their own sample to take home. The beauty in this class lies in the fun everyone will be having – all the while learning about essential oils and Young Living. It shows students how easy it is to create their own recipes at home. This is a social class for sure. Expect people to be exchanging stories, tips, and ideas. It is often best if you are hosting a large class to have help setting this up and monitoring tables to ensure supplies are replenished and in case students have questions.

Fifth, the individual class. This class is perhaps the easiest one for budding leaders to master. Call a friend up and arrange a meeting either in your home or theirs, or perhaps a more neutral location like a coffee shop. Bring your bag of oils, an idea of what you'll be saying, and start sharing. At first glance, this may not seem like a class to you. It is perhaps, one of the best a potential new member can attend. They have your undivided attention and can ask as many questions as they wish. You will, no doubt, be more at ease sharing one-on-one, and can really fit the information you are presenting towards the interests of your student.

The common thread in all of these classes will be the Young Living products. With new members, the best information to start with is the history of Young Living. There are hundreds of essential oil companies in the world. What makes Young Living so special and sets it above the rest? Talk passionately about our history, our numerous farms, and our amazing distilleries. Speak eloquently about our founder, Gary Young, and his history of farming, teaching, and essential discoveries. He is one of the foremost authorities in the world on essential oils. Essential oil research and education are his passion – make them yours. Discuss common errors made by others in the essential oil market: buying from oil brokers instead of planting your own or developing partner farms, having aluminum distillers (aluminum leaches into the plant material), distilling plants for too short a time with too high of heat, or worst of all, adding to the bottle synthetics, chemicals or plants grown with pesticides, weed killers, or other chemicals used during the growing cycle. Make sure to illustrate our "Seed to Seal" commitment. Do you know how many companies can boast an almost thirty-year history of essential oil research and education, nearly a dozen farms and partner farms (increasing in number yearly), and beyond organic growing practices with a commitment guaranteeing that from the smallest seed all the way to the sealed bottle, the company has planted it, nurtured it, distilled it, and bottled it? NONE. Seriously, none. There are companies with a thirty-year history. There are companies which own their own farms. There are companies with their own plants and organic growing practices. There are companies distilling their own oils. There are companies that bottle their own oils. There simply are no companies doing all of these things together, and if any of them came close, they would not have the history, research, and quality commitment Young Living was built upon.

Next, teach about Young Living's membership benefits. We have one of the greatest money saving plans in the industry in our essential rewards program. Membership begins with our Premium Starter Kit. Over the years the oils have changed a bit, only getting better with time, but one thing remains constant – this kit will provide a new member with everything they need to get started. Teach them about the diffuser, the oils in the kit, the samples included, and why they are so amazing. Remember to tell them this kit is an unbelievable value to get them started, and they will have membership with a 24% discount off retail prices for twelve months from the date of last purchase. This is huge. It means they don't have a yearly fee like some programs. Just make a minimum $50 purchase and membership extends another twelve months. It doesn't get much simpler than that! If the Premium Starter Kit does not seem like the right start for them, there are numerous other

Start Living kits and a Basic kit for them to choose from to launch their membership!

It may be difficult for a novice to wrap their mind around the concept of essential oils to support health and wellness. Give them time. You will have some who will sign up immediately, but many more who will need to grow accustomed to the new ideas and information over a few months. Do you remember what it was like for you to learn something new? Chances are, they will be hearing much more about Young Living and essential oils in the next few months. It is like buying a new car. Before you purchased it, you hardly saw it on the road anywhere. After you bought it, your model is everywhere. Did everyone really go out and buy the same model the weekend you did? Nope. You are just more aware of it. Most things in life work this way. We are aware first, then become accustomed to seeing or hearing about something, then we choose to embrace it and learn more, or reject it and stay ignorant on whatever it was we were confronted with in the beginning. Most of us who remember the dawn of readily available Internet felt much the same way. Suddenly, it was in our homes and we had this thing called a home computer – the fashionable thirty-pound desk type variety. We had to make a decision. Learn to utilize this resource or remain in the dark as time and education moved on around us. Most people will choose knowledge. Be there to support, answer questions, and provide research. Remember, you are building a lasting relationship. These things take time and effort to succeed. You cannot print out a hundred pages of research and link them to a dozen webinars and expect anyone to learn. Guiding someone in a new and unfamiliar adventure means you hold their hand, walk them through the steps, and be a friend. Think back to elementary school … there is a reason the teacher put us in pairs during outings, field trips and adventures: life is just more fun with a buddy – and it is harder to get lost with another human being attached to your person.

12

Sprouting Up – Budding Leaders

A garden is a magnificent teacher. It teaches devotion, patience, and hard work. When the lessons have been fully learned and successfully accomplished, the garden will reward you for a lifetime.

Within a few weeks to several months of your first class, you will quite possibly have dozens of members. Among them, a few will end up standing out to you. Either they have indicated they would like to do Young Living as a business, or you have mentioned the possibilities to them and they seem intrigued by the concept of free oils and a paycheck. Tread carefully. No, really – TREAD CAREFULLY. These are *new* business builders. They are most likely overwhelmed with all of the new information, the thought of teaching classes, meeting new people, and sharing their love of Young Living. The last thing you want to do is start micro-managing them in an effort to help. We've all been there before, in the *real* work world. You know, the boss who is really bossy? The one who takes all of your time, gives you a hundred tasks, and then micro-manages all of them? Remember, we are not in a *real* world job for a reason. We don't like the 40-hour work week, and like being our own boss. Let them be their own boss. They need to design their schedule, their goal sheet, and their task list. Whether they meet with one person or twenty is up to them. If they choose to work ten hours a week on Young Living is up to them. Informal or formal style teaching is up to them. Are you getting it, yet? You have zero control over your budding business builders. This is not a business of control. So what is it? A *relationship*. Really, once again, it becomes that simple. As a friend who has done this business successfully, you are then *mentoring* them. Mentoring looks far different than controlling. Friends, as leaders, will mentor; bosses will control.

To build a relationship, you need one main ingredient, sprinkled with a handful of supporting ones. This ingredient is trust. Your budding leaders need to trust you, and know you have their best interests in mind when offering advice or suggestions. If there is no trust, your budding leader may be very hesitant to take a leap of faith into the unknown world of direct marketing. The other ingredients needed are love, respect, and dreams. Trust, love, and respect come only with time spent building a relationship. You cannot manufacture these at will. You must do the time. Be there for the big conversations and life moments. Be there for the little conversations and random moments. *Just be there*. It sounds too simple. You are thinking to yourself right now, "*Sure. Be there. Right. What kind of advice is that?*" It isn't rocket science. Think of the best relationships you have today. What were they built on? Guaranteed it wasn't sharing the same size in clothing. No, you probably have a handful of crazy, zany, I–can't-believe-we-did-that moments, along with a few hair-raising stories where one of you saved the other – even if it was only from walking into a closed glass door at the store, and lastly – *most importantly* – you've got those life changing moments such as a wedding, the birth of a baby, graduation, death, or some other mega-event which you both held onto the thought that the other person was your anchor. Now, realize, not all relationships can be *that* tight. You were meant to walk through this life with a few forever friends. As the saying goes, "They'd help you bury the body and never ask any questions." They are the Thelmas to your Louise. But this doesn't mean you should close out the possibility of new relationships because you

have met your quota. In fact, if you do, you are hurting yourself more than you realize. Life is relationship. Relationship is life. We are defined by our relationships.

With all that in mind, look carefully at your five closest friends. You are the summation of your five closest friends. The old adage, show me your friends and I'll show you your future, is an accurate one. Want to be a Royal Crown Diamond in Young Living? Start building a relationship with your upline immediately. The knowledge, wisdom, and experience they have gained on their journey will greatly help you along on yours – and perchance, you might avoid the mistakes they made in their own business and capitalize on the great ideas they came up with, which will help your organization, too! In looking at your team of budding leaders, keep your mindset on this thought. You want your leaders to emulate your actions. You want them to gain insight from your teachings and ideas. To accomplish this, you must become one of their five closest friends. After all, if they are the summation of their five closest friends and you are among that sacred group of friends, well, they will naturally be more like you.

Hopefully, right about now, you have a few light bulbs glowing as you think through this and wonder how you can begin to cultivate a relationship with both your upline and downline team members. One of the easiest, no fuss, relaxed methods of doing this is to invite them for coffee or tea. There is no need to be formal, or go full throttle preparing an event. A cup of coffee or tea and good conversation. *Just that simple.* If you can't seem to make your schedules work together, give them a call. Nothing beats a good, old-fashioned phone call. Remember back when you were young and you knew all of your friends' phone numbers by heart? If you are in your thirties or forties, you can probably vividly recall flying home from school to hop on the phone to dial your bestie up and tell her all about something amazing. Now, with cell phones in everyone's hand, there really is no more dialing your bestie. Click one button or voice command and he/she is there. Come on. It was so much more difficult back in the day when we had to wait for the dial tone and push all the little square buttons. This is so easy. You really have

no excuse. *Connect* with your people. If you are truly connecting with them, you will see such phenomenal things happening in your teams.

You've probably heard the phrase, "The fortune is in the follow-up" in regards to network marketing businesses. A common misconception for aspiring leaders is the assumption the fortune is actual dollars. Don't misunderstand, a residual income business can yield a veritable fortune, but what needs to be understood here is the fortune is the *relationship*. Through the adventure, guidance, care and love – really getting to know and appreciate your team, you will develop relationships more tightly woven than the roots of the oak tree. There is your fortune. In the end, we are not measured by how much money we have or what we own. We are measured in our relationships – a value truly immeasurable, *simply priceless*.

13

Social Media

*You're frustrated because you keep waiting for the blooming
of flowers of which you have yet to sow the seeds.*
- Dr. Steve Maraboli

If you find yourself with budding leaders who live in another state
– or country – your task is difficult, but not impossible. First of all,
friend them on Facebook. It is amazing how Facebook has made the
world so small; it is all practically in your backyard. Don't use social
media? Better start now. Truly. Certainly, you had your reasons for
not using social media, and for sure they were valid ones. However,
think about this. You are trying to grow a network marketing
business. Social media sites have one – *and only one* – goal: to allow
people to network. Why on earth would you avoid the greatest tool
at your disposal? Now that we have established you must cave in
and use Facebook, start messaging, posting, and commenting. Not
just about Young Living. About your hopes, dreams, and life. Avoid
posting controversial topics such as politics, religion, vaccinations,
or the age-old debate about boxers or briefs. Do not post about what
you had for breakfast, lunch, and dinner and, above all else, don't
post a thousand selfies of yourself having a good hair day. Your posts
should be thoughtful, reflective, uplifting and inspiring, and should
be *relatable*. While Young Living is amazing, and one of the subjects

you like to talk about from the time you get up until you go to bed, remember it can be overwhelming. *Go back to the rule of thirds!* For every one Young Living post you create, post two having nothing to do with Young Living. If you post only business, you will find very quickly you have lost your audience, and people will start ignoring your posts, or worse, *"unfriending"* you. When you are posting about Young Living, keep in mind, people gravitate away from those who sound like car salesmen. Read the difference in these two posts:

> "Young Living essential oils are the best on the planet! We use them everyday and can't get enough of them. Not only have they replaced my old favorites from other companies with their amazing products, they have replaced my husband's income as well. Want to experience health and financial wellness for yourself? I have a voucher worth $20 for the next person who signs up! Call or message me now to find out how! You can also head to youngliving.com and sign up with a Premium Starter Kit today by using my member number, #987654321. What are you waiting for! You will LOVE it!"

> "Oh goodness. I have seriously become addicted to Young Living. I know it hasn't been long, but their products have won me over. We are slowly replacing all of our old chemical laden products with our newer, healthy obsession. It is unbelievable to me the difference we have all seen in our health and wellness. Even Joe has noticed a difference. He no longer feels like falling asleep at his desk after lunch now that he has been taking Multigreens and Ningxia Nitro for the last few weeks. So glad he is not relying on so much coffee! Young Living surprised me this month by giving me the gift of a $20 off voucher to share with a friend. If anyone wants it, just message me and it's yours to use towards your own starter kit. I'd share mine, but between the kids and Joe, it is almost gone. Who knew we'd love them so much?"

See the difference? One is the car salesman hawking a product, the other, a friend sharing. Think about the last thing you tried because a friend shared. Chances are it was a baked good or dinner recipe. We think nothing of sharing a recipe we find online that our family falls in love with, but when it comes to something we make a commission on, we hesitate. Why? With each posting, keep in mind the amazingly delicious Sesame Orange Chicken crockpot recipe your friend shared. She raved about the taste, the scrumptious flavor, the easy preparation in her crockpot while she was at work – the fact that her five-year old picky eater ate every last bite. When you read those words, you saved the recipe, gathered all the ingredients you would need, and put a pot on for yourself. If it worked for her, surely your picky eater would love it, too! Would it have changed your opinion of her chicken testimony if you knew she was being paid a commission to talk about a certain brand of crockpot? Nope. She is your friend. You know she is a beautiful person, trustworthy and kind. You know she would not endorse a product she didn't truly love herself. Why then, do you feel any different sharing Young Living with your friends? *They know you are a beautiful person, trustworthy and kind. They know you would not endorse a product you don't truly love yourself.* Just don't let your fears get ahead of you and prevent you from sharing. Keep in mind the crockpot full of Sesame Orange Chicken. When you compose your post, ask yourself, "*Am I sharing chicken or selling a car?*" The same holds true for your messages with friends. A thoughtful, well-crafted message goes a long way towards your desire to see a friend fall in love with the products and company you know and love.

To build a relationship when separated geographically, only messaging and commenting on their life posts are not enough. You will need to pick up the phone and call them. Many leaders affectionately term these "care calls." The primary goal in these phone calls is to build your relationship. There is no way a person can speak with someone regularly and not learn about their kids and spouse, hardships and triumphs, and their hopes and dreams. Care calls are a way of checking in with a friend. You are *not* calling to sell them oils. You are not calling to talk all about Young Living.

You are not calling to tell them all about *your* life. You are calling to show you *care*. Without a doubt, you will end up talking about oils, supplements, and all things Young Living. You will also end up talking about yourself a bit, so be prepared to share. Mostly, though, you will be listening. Ask an open-ended question such as, "How are things going in your neck of the woods?" *Then listen. Really, really, listen.* Do you know how you ask someone when you pass by, "How are you doing?" and they respond, "Fine, and you?" as they are hurriedly walking past doing a thousand other things, mentally far away from your conversation? Don't be that person who says "fine, and you?" They are showing very clearly they have no time for your answer, but they are being polite by asking. Ask truly wanting an answer, an answer where you have made time to listen and respond. When this is the case, you will learn so much about your friend you did not know. Your relationship with them will blossom into something so very special. Knowing you care enough to call and catch up with them will make them feel valued and appreciated for who they are and, in return, gift you with a friendship which will stand the test of time. It is this *friendship* that will help your business grow. Your friends want to be part of your life. They want to see what makes you who you are, what you are passionate about, and how they can relate to you in your world. This desire inspires them to try Young Living, support you in your ambitions, or even join you in adventures like building a business. Ask any Young Living Diamond and they will introduce you to half a dozen friends in their organization who joined them on the journey and built a business to have fun with their friend.

We've only touched the surface of the support you will need to provide a budding leader. Below are some of the areas you must concentrate on and empower them so they have all the tools for success:

- Teach them how to share the chicken and not the car.

- Break down the compensation plan so they understand.

- Provide them with resources, reference guides, and

information.

- Help them develop a plan for success.

- Meet with them regularly to troubleshoot issues and strategize possibilities.

- Help them teach classes and plan a calendar.

- Be there to listen.

- Build them up when they falter; celebrate them for effort.

14

Mentorship versus Dictatorship

Raise your words, not your voice.
It is rain that grows flowers, not thunder.
- Rumi

In order for you to be successful at empowering them with these things, you must avoid the trap of dictatorship. Think mentorship. You are mentoring them: sharing with them all of the great ideas you have, strategies which worked for you, and offering to support them by arming them with knowledge and resources so they will succeed. What you are not doing is dictating how they should run their organization. It is their business. One of the uniquely great aspects about having a network marketing business is you, and only you, get to decide how to develop it, nurture it, and cultivate it. This being the case, advice, ideas, or plans you may impart to your budding leader may be taken in part, whole, or completely and totally ignored. Be prepared. In the end, it is back to the heart of the matter: it is none of your business how they choose to run their business. Everyone is different and what may work for one person may not work for another. In the same manner, what one desires, another may not. Don't take it as a personal affront to your skills at leadership. Your job as a leader is a job of serving your leaders with humility, integrity, and honesty in all that you do.

If serving is beneath you, leadership is above you. Leadership is not about you, it is about the one you are leading. After all, there can be no leadership without someone to lead, right?

What truly defines a great leader?

Well, let's break it down to the very basics, the definition. Merriam Webster's dictionary defines the word lead as a verb meaning: to guide someone or something along the way or to guide a dance partner through the steps of a dance.

Notice neither of the above definitions say to push, pull, poke, prod, or cajole someone along the way. As leaders, we should be the very personification of those definitions. We are to guide. The second definition is especially appropriate to what we should be doing. This journey is a partnership whereby both you and your budding leader should be "dancing" together through the rehearsed steps you have taught them so they can succeed. Only in doing this together, will you see them grow and mature as a leader. You have done this awhile, and know the steps to take. Someone new will be relying on you to teach them all of the steps needed. Take your job seriously. You are not just letting yourself down when you fail to make the effort and give fully of your time, talent, and leadership. You are letting your team down. While we sometimes want to be "in charge,"— and there is a time and a place for this – it is often a far better friendship and business practice to mentally lock away your inner dictator and practice your two-step instead.

15

Pollination - Be Duplicatable

You cannot expect your team to rise above your example.
- Orrin Woodward

Have you ever been around one of those people? You know, the kind who does everything and does it perfectly? The one who is beyond organized, volunteers for everything, has a perfectly kept house and family, and somehow manages to show up to everything looking beautiful? You want to hate her. But you love her. You might secretly want to be like her. You just don't think you've got what it takes. So instead of try, you put on your yoga pants and sneakers and head out the door. Why is that? What has she got, that you have not? Seriously. Think about that? The answer, surprisingly, is nothing. You have all the right stuff to be just like her if you really wanted to be. The problem is, she has made it look like an unattainable art form. You just know she has a superhuman secret power that morphs her from average mom to a blonde, powerhouse bombshell, reminiscent of June Cleaver and Martha Stewart rolled into one. You'd sooner grow a third leg than be able to accomplish that unattainable feat! Here is the thing: she has made it look completely and totally not duplicable by any stretch of your imagination. So you do not even try.

As leaders, we can learn to two-step – and even tango if need be – doing everything right with our team, guiding our partners through the world of network marketing and team building... but – and this is a BIG but – if you have not made yourself and your actions look duplicable, no one will duplicate your efforts. When you step away, even for a moment, and your budding leader has to take a new partner to two-step with, they will falter, step all over toes, and ultimately, walk away from the dance.

How do I make myself duplicable, you ask? Well, to start with, share all of your tips and secrets for saving time, organizing your business and life, and taking care of your team. Share both your successes and failures so they can learn from both. Show your leader that the "Great and Powerful Oz" was just an ordinary person behind a curtain. If you make everything seem like smoke and mirrors, the illusion will stun them. They will assume only you have this unique gift of leadership and business. They need to see you working through things. They must learn the work involved, the time saving secrets you have figured out, and how to repeat your steps on the path to success without having you pulling or pushing them along with your efforts. Once again, by making each leader a friend, growing a relationship and partnership with them, you are guiding their efforts – you need to keep it simple, uncluttered, and manageable. Ask yourself when implementing new ideas, "Is this duplicable or overwhelming?" If the answer is overwhelming, consider if it is worth it to continue. Some things, you will do anyway, because they are unique just to you and your personality and business, but most ideas and implementations, which are not duplicable, need to be revised so they are so.

One of the greatest downfalls for you will be if you are not duplicable, everyone will come to you for the answers. At first, with a dozen or so leaders, it might make you feel special... like the President feels special. However, after awhile, when your team grows to epic proportions and you have hundreds of leaders all looking to you for answers, you will feel more like a prisoner than the President. By setting realistic expectations for your team, and showing them step-by-step how to implement them and manage their own classes, organization, and challenges, you are not only empowering them for total success, you are freeing yourself from a lifetime of self-inflicted incarceration in the "I'm-Just-Not-Duplicable Penitentiary." Empower your leaders and they will lead.

16

Time Spent in the Garden

The glory of gardening: hands in the dirt, head in the sun,
heart with nature. To nurture a garden is to feed not
just the body, but the soul.
- Alfred Austin

I f you tend to your leaders, like flowers in a garden, they will surely bloom. Just like a garden, there will be thorns, weeds, and it can get dirty. This is just part of life. Some leaders, like plants, will suffer from failure to thrive despite your best attempts. With your guidance and care, the majority will flourish and produce many offshoots and blossoms. As a gardener of leaders, you need balance. Too much water, a plant dies. Too little water, the same. Your leaders need to have your time and attention. They need to have the nutrients you provide, and the support you give them. Conversely, they do not need too much of these things. Balance means everything for you and for them. Give them enough to get them started, show them how to grow, then step back and allow them space to do so. Think about the mighty oak tree. It can grow upwards of 50 to 75 feet tall and live 100-300 years, weighing on average 7-12 tons. Not much can sway the mighty oak tree. Yet, it all began with the tiniest acorn, weighing less than an ounce. Like a young oak sapling, your leaders can be bent or broken based on the harsh environment or your negligent treatment. With you as a supporting rod, they can weather any storm. With time comes deepening roots to hold it firmly in place, a strong trunk to bear the weight of the many branches, and a bounty of future acorns to grow more trees. Be the support now, and they will become like an indomitable oak tree in the future and become a solid and mighty leader.

Conversely, you need to allow the oak tree space to grow. If you confine it by closing it in tight, always pruning and pricking, shaping it in the way you choose for it to grow, you will end up with a miniature oak bonsai, unable to bear any real weight or stress. A bonsai-shaped leader will depend on you for everything, and will be unable to grow outside of its planter. The greatest gardeners also look to the plant for advice on how to help it thrive. Ask your leaders how you can support them best. Work with them through issues, avoiding the common pitfall of taking care of the issue for them. If you always take care of the issue, they will never know how to handle it down the road when it is their turn to help someone else.

17

The Forgotten Family

More than any seed of opportunity,
relationship seeds will yield the greatest harvest.

As with any passion, we can become so entrenched in pursuit and enjoyment, we neglect many things around us requiring time and attention as well. For a great leader, often, it is family, friends, and personal activities that get placed on the back burner. Our intentions are good, for sure. We think to ourselves, "if I could just do this one more thing..." or "a few more hours, and I'll have it done!" This mentality is self-defeating and a detriment to your family's health and happiness. What kind of example are we setting for our children if we are always working or thinking about work? To maintain a happy family and prevent exhaustion from taking over, you must prioritize and focus on creating balance. One way to do this is to list your key areas where time should be spent. Next, take out your calendar and fill in the next three months. Yes, the next THREE months. You won't need all the details. Right now, you are just focusing on tasks. Grab your highlighters. You will need three colors. For this example, let's go with yellow, orange, and blue. Your assignment is to look at each week. Where can you fit family time? You need at least one day of dedicated family time. It doesn't need to be the entire day – though nice if it is! – but it needs to be quality time. Outline or color in the square each week with the color you have dedicated to family. It can be a different day each week. If you know details, such as maybe a day hiking around the lake, or biking through local trails, maybe just going to a local event or heading out for a movie and pizza with dessert at your favorite shop, write them down. It doesn't need to be big, fancy, or expensive. Your family just wants you – any way they can get you. Business will always be available. Family will not. Your children are growing up and will soon be gone. You will never hear a man dying say he wished he had spent more time at the office, but you will hear them often lament they spent so much time away from their loved ones. Business is great – be passionate, be invested, give it all you've got – but for a period of time, a season, a set schedule, a concrete section of time. Do not let it consume you.

Now that you have four/five days of family time in each month, look at where you can schedule classes, meeting, events, or other business. If you are working Young Living as a part-time business, this could be simple and easy. If you are full-time, it may take some impressive manipulation of your schedule to figure this one out. Once there, color or outline those squares in your chosen business color. Lastly, look at what is left. On one of those days, you must schedule something just for you and your spouse. Again, it mustn't be an extravagant trip or expensive dinner date. Just time. Time for two people who love and adore one another to... well... love and adore one another. A picnic, movie, dinner, romantic walk, adventure, or simply a quiet evening alone. You need this. Your spouse needs this. Quite often, our kids take a backseat to our business, and our poor spouse gets the trunk of the car. You know, you only look in there when you are missing something for a long while. Don't let your marriage become a threesome with a business affair. After you have outlined or colored those days in your chosen romance color, look at what's left. If there are days left, feel free to schedule them with whatever. It is, after all, your calendar. Taking the time to do this important task will ensure you actually still have a family a decade from now when you are a Royal Crown Diamond.

Life and business are simply a balancing act. Think of a scale. When you place more weight in the work section, the family side of the scale gets lighter, or vice versa. You need to keep a healthy balance between the two. Avoid over-extending yourself, taking on too many tasks, which do not require you, specifically, to tackle them. If you have led your team effectively, you have competent leaders who should be managing the bulk of their own issues and teams. Don't be like the clown in the circus juggling four plates, then five, then ten. By the end, he is exhausted, and chances are, he has dropped several of them. You have three plates on your calendar that must be juggled. Just three. If you choose to add in church activities, local groups, volunteering, outside projects, etc. – that is entirely up to you. Just realize, with each plate comes a greater challenge and risk for failure. Some will need to be dropped occasionally or be passed to a partner so you can effectively manage the load. No one, not even Ringling or PT Barnum, himself, can find someone great enough to juggle fifty plates. You won't impress anyone with your juggling skills and will shatter all of your precious plates.

18

Time Management

Liberty, when it begins to take root,
is a plant of rapid growth.
-George Washington

Y ou are not a doctor. You are not on-call. Ever. Remember that. Sometimes, in our efforts to be the greatest leader we can be, we sacrifice family time, meals – even sleep – in an effort to lead our team. This is not beneficial to you, your family, or your team. First, you are going to destroy your family. Yes, you read that right. Destroy. There is a reason so many medical professionals in this country are divorced. They eat, sleep, and breathe their work, and there is nothing left for anyone else. It will consume you. Second, you will destroy your team. Now, you are wondering: "how? If I am putting all of my time and energy into something, how on earth can I destroy it?" You are showing your leaders to give up everything, like you are doing, to grow their teams. They will emulate your methods and grow bitter and disillusioned over time. Some will look at you and your frazzled life and say it isn't worth it to even start a Young Living business if the result is they become like you. It simply is not duplicable. Here is the thing. You cannot be all things to all people. Once you start realizing that fact, and preparing yourself and your leaders to do the best you can, when you can, and let people learn to take care of themselves when the issue warrants, you will begin to have time to relax … maybe even get a shower or go to the bathroom without the phone ringing. In essence, what we are discussing here is time management. If you do not manage your time, it will manage you. Show your leaders, and your family, how to successfully manage their time by being a shining example of this yourself.

19

Fantasy and Reality

Every failure contains within it the seeds
for wisdom and growth.
- Amanda Uribe

W hen analyzing our expectations of ourselves, our family, and our business, we need to be sure to keep a large, healthy dose of reality in the mix. All too often, we get caught up in the dream phase of building a business. Our expectations are set high, and while admirable, can ultimately lead to our downfall. Having an unrealistic expectation will result in your crushing disappointment if you fail to make the goal. Look at the compensation plan. It does not start with Star and then show Diamond as the next rank. In fact, the compensation plan is broken down into three very specific and attainable sections. You must adjust your goals to be realistic in size, achievable within a realistic period, enough to challenge you to work hard, but not so much of a challenge you will fall flat on your face.

To do this:

- set specific, realistic, measureable goals.

- break larger undertakings into smaller amounts.

- set a realistic timeline for achieving goals.

- tell someone your goals, everyone needs an accountability partner to motivate them.

- keep your eyes focused on the finish line.

When listing out your goals, think about what, exactly, it will take to achieve them. Grow your garden with these thoughts in mind. Do not look at grow as a verb, but rather an acronym for your actions.

G – GOALS – what are you trying to achieve?

Short-term goals

Long-term goals

End result of entire growing process?

Timeline for your finished garden?

How can you break down the growth?

How can you sustain the growth?

Is it challenging enough, but not overwhelming?

Have you set realistic time and growth expectations?

R – Reality Check – is it a fanciful notion or a possible outcome?

How much is in your control versus what relies on the team?

What results have you produced so far?

What results has your team produced so far?

What is the current situation?

What environmental factors are present?

Is your timeline reasonable?

O – Obstacles – what is getting in the way of success?

Are you your own obstacle? Others?

What other issues may be present?

If so, how can you navigate around them?

What choices do you have and what are their benefits?

Are they cost effective or prohibitive?

What might you have to sacrifice to achieve this goal? Is the sacrifice worth the reward?

W – Which way? At the fork in the road, left or right?

What actions do you need to take immediately?

What actions can you plan ahead?

Is this a team action, or just yourself?

Will these actions produce duplicable results?

Who should help out and support these efforts?

Each section of the compensation plan should be an individual plan of attack. Remember how to eat the elephant? One bite at a time. This doesn't mean neglect planning for the structure needed for Royal Crown Diamond. Absolutely plan. Just don't obsess about the entire thing. If you look at the last section, you will see you reach your goal with six teams of business builders (legs), each having 35,000 personal group volume and your entire team having an overall gross volume of 1.5 million in sales per month. A truly daunting prospect for anyone. Obsessing over that day in and day out would drive someone insane. Know the end goal. Then look in front of it. Break it down and determine how long you feel it should take you to reach this goal. Three years, five years, ten. The choice is yours. It is your business, your timeline. Do not let anyone tell you differently. Success looks different to everyone, and only *you* can define your success.

Remember, this is a marathon, not a sprint. You *will* cross the finish line if you so choose, and when you do, you will not care how long it took you to get there, just that you did. There is a wonderful story about one of the Olympic runners from Zimbabwe. His name was Stephen Akwari. Sent to run for his country in 1969 in the Mexico Olympic games, he was quickly injured while running, but trudged on, determined to finish. Miles and miles later, limping, in extreme pain, and still many hours from the finish, the race was over and people were heading home. He was still running. People told him the race was over. People told him to give up. People told him he was finished. He kept running as if his life's blood depended on it. When he crossed the finish line, with few people even left there to see him do so, he was asked by a reporter why he bothered when he knew the race was long since over. His response was probably one of the greatest responses ever to such a question. The exhausted response: "*My country did not send me to start a race. My country sent me to finish a race.*" This is your personal business marathon. How fast you run, how many people you beat to Royal Crown Diamond, how perfectly you teach and lead as well as the next guy, or whether or not you make a few mistakes while growing are irrelevant. How you started and never gave up is what your friends, family, and team will cheer for when you reach the goal. How you handled it all with faith, integrity, optimism, and grace is what they will remember long after you have made it.

Many longtime builders agree, after attaining Executive, a rank each year or two is a great, realistic goal. This is not to say you have to do this. It is true, some leaders have gone from member to Royal Crown Diamond in a couple short years. As we have established, you are your own boss. Make the determination and go for it. You and you alone know what you are capable of achieving, but do remember you have a team to think of, as well. If they all share your "shoot to the moon" attitude, you might be able to speed up the ranking timeline. Be wise in assessing your goals, though. It might be easy for a prior network marketing professional or someone with a large network of friends, family, and coworkers to grow quickly. It will be more difficult for someone without these elements. Not impossible. Just more difficult.

Having a firm idea of the goal, look now at the first section of the compensation plan: Star through Executive ranks. Study the requirements, post them on your refrigerator. Create a G.R.O.W. plan detailing how you intend to reach the end goal of this manageable section: Executive. Once you have your plan, put it into action. Color code your calendar with your family, spouse, and work days. As we've discussed, a class or meeting once a week is ideal. Do more or less depending on your needs and desires. In the beginning, it is best to make a couple of lists. The first one, a list of all the friends and family you feel fairly certain would be interested in a great company with phenomenal products. The second list, those friends or acquaintances you are less certain about, but want to speak with, sharing your love of Young Living and your "why". After you have your plan in place, start with the first list. For two reasons, this will be a great starting point. First, your close friends and family genuinely love and appreciate you. They want to support your endeavors and passions. When they see how much you adore this company and your essential oils, and know you would never endorse a product you do not believe in for your family, they will most likely be intrigued and come around to the idea of membership and an oil starter kit of their very own. Second, you will feel far more confident approaching all of your acquaintances after you have practiced on your family and friends. Remember, you aren't trying to sell them a car they don't need. Think Sesame Orange Chicken. Share. Don't Sell. You are helping them join a company providing health and wellness support for their entire family. Truly, you are doing them the greatest disservice by withholding this information.

20

Rising Star Team Bonus

From a small seed a mighty trunk may grow.
- Aeschylus

In looking at this first section of the compensation plan, you will notice a section at the bottom on "Rising Star Team Bonus." This is a neat little bonus you should be striving to achieve every month. If you look closely at the requirements, you will notice the design of this bonus sets you up for all six legs needed to make Royal Crown Diamond in the future. It even gives you a seventh leg should something happen to compromise one of your other legs – a substitute leg. Early on in your business, this bonus will be phenomenal for a few reasons. First, you will be getting a nice chunk of bonus money by attaining some pretty simple and realistic goals. Second, you will be able to use this money to start investing in supplies and products necessary to run your business. This money allows you to avoid breaking into your savings account to start up a business. Brilliant. Third, you will be learning how to strategize possible placements of team leaders and help them develop dynamic teams of their own. You are eligible every single month for this bonus from the first time the requirements are met until you make Silver, or twenty-four months have gone by – whichever comes first. You are thinking this sounds great, but what's the catch?

There isn't one. Mary Young, Gary's wife, in her infinite wisdom (she knows her way around a compensation plan!) wanted to ensure you had all the right tools at your disposal, the funds to begin, and the right strategy to get you started, so she created the Rising Star Team Bonus (RSTB). Bless her. Her efforts have yielded so many diamonds in this company, and you too, will be one of them if you follow the design of the RSTB and give it your all!

The details of the first requirement:

Establish your first three legs. This is as simple as three people who sign up with membership, sign up with 100pv on Essential Rewards, and have an overall group volume (OGV) of 300 each. There are no hidden requirements. It can be as simple as one of them actually placing a 300pv order, or having a small team under them purchasing a total amount of 300pv. Notice, though, the 100pv order must be on Essential Rewards. Having these three legs with this structure will yield a bonus commission of $50 for one share of the RSTB. Sounds too simple, right? Glad you think so.

Now look at the second requirement:

Develop another two legs while maintaining the first three. Think about that sentence for a minute and don't jump ahead just yet. Three legs (any three) must still meet the first RSTB requirements. Now you need an additional two legs. Each one needs to have 100pv on essential rewards and an overall group volume of 500pv. Once again, there are no stipulations of how this needs to be comprised. It can be a leg of ten people placing small orders or a few people placing larger orders. You've just captured two more bonus shares of $50 each. So, in summation, you have three shares with total value of $150.

Look at the last requirement to capture all shares of the RSTB:

Grow another two legs (for a total of seven) with two legs at overall group volume of 1000 each. Both of them must be on Essential Rewards purchasing a minimum of 100pv. Note once again, you must have the initial five-leg structure with all the requirements discussed thus far. Also note, these do not have to be the same legs you began with initially. It may well be your original leg of 300pv is now your leg of 1000pv and another leg has made it to 300pv. You have now captured the remaining three shares ($50 each) of the RSTB, for a grand total of $300.

Once again, this can be done each month, and is in addition to your regular commission. By structuring your downline to grow seven legs, and supporting those legs to each grow their own seven using the RSTB plan, you are building future diamonds. Young Living truly made it simple and fun to start growing a team without any of the crazy costs, which are usually associated with starting a business.

21

A Faster Start

If you want to be happy for a lifetime, be a gardener.
- Chinese Proverb

Another great idea Young Living incorporated into the compensation plan is the "Fast Start Bonus." Pretty much exactly what it sounds like, this bonus helps you get a faster start towards commission and success! The idea is simple, yet brilliant: when a new member signs up you receive 25% commission for the first three months of their membership! Your jaw dropped, didn't it? Yes, it's true. A whopping 25% commission on the pv of anything they purchase as long as you have purchased a minimum of 50pv yourself. If this wasn't enough of a fast start, they tied the actual sign up of a Premium Starter kit – or any premium kit valued at 100pv – to a "Kit Bonus" of $25. This equates to their first month's sign up with a 100pv Premium Starter Kit yielding $50. Now, it gets even more interesting if you like math. If you have a purchase of 100pv yourself, then you are entitled to an extra bump in money. You see, they pay an additional 8% (the regular unilevel commission) on 30% of the first order.

There's more. Seriously. So, if your sign up goes on to sign up someone else, you receive 10% commission for the first three months on that new member's pv before receiving the regular unilevel commission of 5% from the fourth month and thereafter. This happens with every sign up they get!

Important notes on these bonuses:

- You mustn't be on Essential Rewards yourself to get them, but as we have discussed, being on Essential Rewards just makes sense!

- Their first month is the sign up month, so if they sign up on the last day of the month, technically, they have two months of remaining purchases yielding 25%.

- There is a limit to the fun: maximum 25% earnings are $200per month so if they order 3,000pv in essential oils, you are getting $200 and maximum 10% earnings are $80.

22

Roots Deepen

*A leader's attitude is caught more quickly by followers
than by his or her actions.*

The magnificence of accomplishing the Rising Star Team Bonus and Fast Start Bonus is not the financial windfall every month. Rather, it is the established roots taking hold and growing deeper and deeper in your organization. With every leader you teach to grow a structured team, you are creating new roots and strengthening the existing ones. This width and depth in your team will rapidly develop into not only all the requirements you need to make Royal Crown Diamond, but those for your teammates, too. It becomes a powerhouse of successful leaders growing organizations within the larger organization. The old adage, "Help others achieve their dreams, and yours will come true." is absolute perfection in its candid honesty. Your primary goal as a leader is not to be Royal Crown Diamond. It is to help others achieve this aspiration. After all, if you help a dozen friends make it all the way to Royal Crown Diamonds in your team, didn't you realize your dream, as well? As a leader, you must think outside yourself. No one is an ocean unto themselves. Especially not in a relationship based business. You must have a team spirit or you won't make it.

Strategy in Growth

You must plant many seeds to get a good harvest.

If you look at the compensation plan, it is structured in tiers. Leaders with groups of other leaders with groups. These "teams" are vital to growing in a relationship network marketing business. How you grow these teams has been and will always be the source of much speculation and opinion. Ask a dozen Royal Crown Diamonds how to structure your organization, and you will surely get a dozen different answers. The truth is there really is no right answer. Let's look at a few possible scenarios.

Organic Growth

One of the best ways to grow your business is through organic growth. In theory, this means everyone who comes to Young Living signs up with a friend, and that friend becomes their enroller and sponsor. So let's say Amy teaches a class where fifteen people attend. Amy invited five and they brought their friends. At the end of the night, ten of them become members. When Amy goes to sign everyone up, she signs up the friends she invited, listing herself as enroller and sponsor. The friends she did not invite who are signing up will be listed under the friend who brought them as enroller and sponsor. So, let's say Amy is enroller and sponsor on Emily, but Emily brought Rebecca so she will be listed as enroller and sponsor on her. Clear as mud? Here is the concept: Amy did not invite those ten other friends who attended. They never would have signed up if it was not for Emily, who shared and brought them to class, therefore, they should be listed under her. Organic growth is a method of growing where God plants you. There isn't much strategy there with the exception of maybe zoning in on a leg needing more OGV and hosting classes or offering incentives directed towards that line. The benefit of this type of growth is the relationship is already most likely established. They could be family friends, church friends, or know each other through various community connections. This prior relationship allows an immediate camaraderie between the two of them with this new adventure. If Rebecca has questions, knowing Emily already, she will feel perfectly comfortable asking them. If and when Rebecca decides to start Young Living as a business, she and Emily will be amazing together. They will rely on their shared friendship to fortify their businesses, and enjoy a great adventure together. There isn't a much better method than building this business with a friend.

Strategic Growth

Strategic growth is much harder to navigate with sometimes murky waters. The concept is simple. Look at the leaders you have growing in your organization. You will surely find someone giving it their all and dedicating 100% all the time towards growing a business. You would zone in on them and help them establish a team. Let's say you host a class and ask one of your leaders to help out. Ten people attend. For our example, our leader, Megan is struggling. She is doing everything right, but for whatever reason, things just are not falling into place. When four people sign up at the class, you determine it is a good strategy to place them in Megan's team. She needs to grow her team and you, as her leader and mentor, are helping her do so. By your own estimate, you certainly do not need to grow any wider, but you do need depth in your lines. Helping Megan will help you and her to grow. It will create a tighter bond between you both because you are going to take on these new sign ups as a team with Megan as their immediate upline and you as the team lead and mentor.

Many great leaders choose strategic placement of their team members so they can help budding leaders develop teams and help them gain a strong foundation. As a leader, you want nothing more than to see your team members experience the same growth and excitement you feel growing your teams. By helping them gain new members on their team and helping those new members find and grow their teams, too, you are creating very strong teams within teams. In essence, you are creating a solid foundation.

With strategic placement, it can also sometimes be a gamble. No one really knows which members will fall in love with their oils and sign up for Essential Rewards, or which ones will jump into the business. There will be times where someone signs up for Essential Rewards right away, and asks a ton of business questions, but this is rare. Most people need to ease into the interesting but unknown garden of essential oils. You will need to make certain your team leader who is gaining these new members wants them, will support and build a relationship with them, and will take care of them. If you are not certain your team leader can do this, then do not even think for a second of putting someone in their team. New members deserve our best. Time, attention, and love. Very simple elements – if we can't give them freely and with abundance, we are doing a disservice to our members. Just like seedlings need continual care and attention, so do new members and budding leaders. The larger your garden, the more difficult a task you have ahead of you.

Now, some of you may be thinking about now, "I will never strategically place someone, it is just too much work." Okay. Maybe you won't. But what would you do if you saw your best friend lose a leg when a business leader who is struggling steps away from Young Living? What if the loss of this leg meant she was going to lose her rank and you were going to lose the OGV you needed to maintain yours because of this? By scheduling a few quick classes and placing the sign ups in her team, you could help both of you maintain your rank, and possibly develop another dynamic team for both of you. Would you do it then? Maybe you would. Maybe you would not. The choice is ultimately yours.

Let's be perfectly clear on two things. Number one: you placed these friends of yours into Megan's frontline. It is up to you to ensure a relationship is fostered between them so the new member knows both you and Megan are taking care of them and they feel comfortable going to Megan with questions. Number two: you are team building in this scenario. Make sure, a million percent sure, you are doing this for the right reasons. Make sure it is about Megan and helping her develop a dynamic team of her own. Placing a sign up on Megan's frontline is far different than getting your next ten sign ups and sticking them one under the other under Megan. That is very near the definition of stacking for pay and rank purposes, which is against the Policies and Procedures of our company and is, quite frankly, a breach of ethics. Ten sign ups from an event can absolutely go under Megan, if – and only if – you are helping her build a dynamic team. If your sole goal is to gain rank and pay, you need to step back and reassess why you are in Young Living to begin with and what your "why" was in the beginning of your journey. Any reason, other than to help a self-motivated leader cultivate a team of their own, shows that you are doing it for the wrong reason.

Exceptions

You will find exceptions to these practiced methods in a very few, unique circumstances. For example, many business builders are also running successful blogs on the Internet. Imagine if you will, how difficult it is to offer a special sign up deal to a readership in the thousands and have three hundred people sign up. Where would you put them? Who would take care of them? There is no way you can take care of two hundred people on your frontline. In an effort to ensure all members are taken care of and have someone to answer all of their newbie questions, you put them in your teams across your frontline. After all, these leaders have shown they are quite capable of managing their own teams and can handle a bit of extra growth and the challenge of looking after a handful of new members. If you were to leave them all across your frontline, three hundred people would now be messaging you, emailing you, and calling you – can you imagine the nightmare this would be for you and those new members? Shudder. Better to think like a leader and use your wisdom to place new members in teams.

Many Young Living leaders successfully use a mix of both organic and strategic methods to grow their teams. Certainly, there is no one-size fits all approach to handling new sign ups in your organization. Be cautious of the advice from leaders who will tell you there is one way, and only one way, to grow. This well-intentioned advice often comes from leaders who have either only grown their entire line organically, or have grown entirely with strategy. Sometimes, the advice will come from someone who tried both methods in their own organization and had a bad experience or a team that failed using a method. Remember, you and your garden are unique. No other garden will look like yours. It is up to you and you alone to decide what methods work for you and your teammates. Each member is also different and their needs are different. Be sure to put a lot of thought into what your planned method of placement is for a new sign up. Regardless of where they are in your organization, or what method brought them there, make certain they know they can come to you for support and leadership.

24

Enroller or Sponsor?

Always do your absolute best,
for what you do now you will harvest later.

Now is a great time to talk about enrollers and sponsors. By now you know when you enroll someone in Young Living under your member number, you are listed as their enroller and sponsor. What does it all mean? Well, as the enroller, as long as you have a personal order of 50pv, you receive the bonuses. On a new sign up with a Premium Start Living kit of 100pv, you will be receiving the $25 Start Living Bonus and 25% Fast Start commission. The sponsor, while they do receive a few dollars in commission off this order and during the first three months, truly sees their commission come around month four. When the three-month Fast Start period is over, they will be receiving 8% commission for the lifetime of the enrollee's membership. If you are the enroller and sponsor, you have no worries here with the exception of being sure to place your 100pv order to receive full commissions each month.

If, however, you have chosen to strategically place a team member in a different level under a budding leader, you have two choices. Give them enroller and sponsor so all monies go to them, or keep the enroller spot for yourself so you receive the bonus money and place them as sponsor so they will receive the 8% commission. There is no wrong answer here. Honestly. Some give away both so they can inspire a new business builder and help them get a great start. Others expect the business builder will be gaining their own sign ups as well, and 8% is still a great commission. Think about what is right for you, your leaders, and your team. Then make the decision you feel is right for you.

25

Growing Wealth

If your actions inspire others to dream more, learn more,
do more, and become more, you are a leader.
- John Quincy Adams

Now, there are some people out there in this big, wide world who are averse to growing wealth. Perhaps you are one of them. Why on earth would anyone not want money? Yes, we've all heard, money is the root of all evil, money is the downfall of man, money is a lonely bedfellow. Really though, think about it. With more money, you can help more people. Money is just money. Nothing more, nothing less. It is what you choose to do with it that may be in question. What the world truly needs is more money in the hands of good people. Think about it for a moment. Have you ever noticed what good people do with their money? God's work. They feed the hungry. They pay for shelters for the cold. They mission to the sick. They help the world's downtrodden and misfortunate souls whom no one else will help. They use their money to change the world, one person at a time, one village at a time. Albert Pine said it best, "What we do for ourselves dies with us, what we do for others and the world remains and is immortal." Yes, the world certainly needs more good people with money. What will you do with yours?

If you are serious about becoming a Royal Crown Diamond with Young Living, you need to figure out this one. Chances are, when you make it, you will have more money than you know what to do with, so have a plan. Collecting millions of acorns from your mighty oak trees with nowhere to store them, no one to share them with, and no plan of greatness will leave you standing there with your garden wheelbarrow trying desperately to figure it all out as the acorns rain down upon your head. With great wealth comes great responsibility. The world needs more money in the hands of good people: you are equal to the challenge.

To attain this wealth, you will be focusing on your leaders and your teams. Their paychecks depend on you teaching them how to be duplicable and how to encourage members to try Young Living's Essential Rewards program. This autoship program inspires new members to collect more oils they will love while getting back credit for future oils, and better than this, some of Young Living's specials are Essential Rewards members exclusive bonuses. These are often oils, supplements, or home care products they may not have tried already. This program is truly wonderful and most members fall in love with it. Having a minimum of one third (back to that rule of thirds!) of your members on Essential Rewards will ensure a steady long-term paycheck. The rest of your paycheck is determined through a unilevel commission program where you earn percentages based on the levels in your organization, and by earning additional commission shares based on how effective you are at growing leaders. Let's take a brief look at how this is set up:

You will notice as an Executive, on your level one, you are earning a commission of 8% on the personal volume purchased. Level two, you will earn 5% and on level 3-5, you will earn 4%. As you increase in rank along the compensation plan, you will notice you get paid the same unilevel commission. What is added on from Silver through Royal Crown Diamond is a series of generational shares and bonuses. The value of these shares change slightly as they are 6.25% percent of Young Living's overall sales, divided among those who qualify. Imagine now, as a Silver, Gold, Platinum or Diamond leader yourself if the Silver Leadership Bonus share was worth $150 and you have 20 Silvers in your first few levels. You just made an extra $3,000 in your paycheck. All because you loved, guided, mentored, and supported twenty people in their hopes and dreams to become a Young Living Silver by helping them grow a successful garden. That isn't all. You may also receive an additional 2.5/3% commission on the personal volume of those legs depending on where they are structured. Pretty amazing, right? It pays to support your people. No good deed goes unrewarded in the garden of Young Living.

26

Building a Team

To be rooted is perhaps the most important
and least recognized need of the human soul.
- Simone Weil

Well, by now you've got deepening roots, probably a fair understanding of The Rising Star Team Bonus, Fast Start, Essential Rewards, and the Compensation Plan, so you are no doubt wondering about the best way to start molding your people into an energetic and motivated team. One of the best ways to begin is to name your team! Sounds pretty easy, right? Think again. Not only are hundreds of teams out there roaming around with a name you probably want, but you also have to look at what other organizations have for names. You wouldn't want the name Earthly Essentials if you found out it belongs to a group of nudists promoting their line of skin firming cream with this name and a logo of a silhouette nude no more than you would want to name your team Heaven's Bounty only to discover it is the name of a famous burlesque show in Las Vegas. Research, research, research. When you find the name you wish to use, start a Facebook business group for disseminating information and promotions to your members far and wide and to allow them to connect with each other. Locally, host business meetings once or twice a month. There, you will discuss

Young Living news, team plans and calendars, recognize your team's efforts, and troubleshoot issues.

Create a logo! This is the fun part. You get to design – or if you are lacking in art talent, pay someone – a logo to identify your team at meetings and around the Young Living world during events. This may seem like a step you can skip, and perhaps if you fall into a much larger, already established and well-identified team, you might get away without it; but truly, your people want to unite as a team and nothing else says team spirit better than a great name, a beautiful logo, and a unified purpose. Solidarity in the garden creates a beautiful landscape. Just leave enough room for your budding leaders to do the same with their individual teams. No room in the garden for a giant ego telling everyone they have to be part of one team only. At Young Living, it isn't my team, your team, their team, or ours. It is one team. One giant garden filled with the best essential oils on the planet. As with any garden, plots get subdivided and grow differently. This is to be expected. It is what makes a garden so colorful, diverse, and vibrant.

Like any massive garden, it takes many gardeners to ensure the best nutrients, care, and attention are given to the plants. Do not bristle or take offense if your budding leaders get something they need to learn and grow from another gardener. Perhaps the gardener tending them has more experience with certain nutrients, or may simply just enjoy the company of the gardener. As one unified garden, we are all in this together. Just as any great team, we all have different talents. Be sure to allow all members to bring their talent into the garden. Be sure to acknowledge these efforts. People want to be needed, appreciated, and recognized and will work harder to hear those words of praise.

Offer business building promotions and challenges to your team. Everyone loves a good challenge so be sure to make it challenging, but not overwhelming and impossible. The best building promotions are often challenges, which inspire them to do things they should be doing as a leader anyway, but often get lost through the cracks while tackling everything else waiting to be accomplished. Offering incentives to leaders who get a certain number of sign ups or Essential Rewards members in a given period is a phenomenal way to encourage growth. Hosting a challenge where leaders are required to make care calls, host classes, and touch base with members is a great way to ensure your members are being taken care of while helping your leaders learn about business and leadership skills.

In all you do, make certain, absolutely certain, you are fostering a team spirit. Every rank you earn depends on your team as a whole, with all of your effort and love behind them in support, and your knowledge and wisdom in front offering guidance. When you achieve a new rank, celebrate them. It is as much their rank as it is yours. The old saying about recognition holds true: "babies cry for it, and grown men die for it." All of us strive for recognition. It is inherent in our very nature. Be sure, however, your recognition is genuine and deserved. A basketful of empty praises is worth about as much as a bucketful of aphids in the garden.

Another excellent way to foster team spirit is to host events together. Whether you are planning an ordinary class or an extraordinary vendor event, these are wonderful opportunities to get everyone working and learning together. It is at these times, we will see our unique personalities blossom as we try new things, gain insight we did not have before, or teach others from our experience. Team events also give you, as a leader, the opportunity to see who, among your team, is truly putting their heart and soul into Young Living. It is those rare individuals giving everything they've got to the team whom you should be investing much of your individual leadership time. Mentoring them will ensure success for both of you.

This isn't to say you should not invest in those who are giving less than their best. Quite often, life goes in seasons and we have seasons where we are super busy and performing well, and others where we are perhaps not working at our full potential. Life also throws us a few curve balls now and again, so our focus and energy may be elsewhere. Certainly lead anyone with a desire to learn and grow.

They are the future of Young Living and it is your job to nurture them until they develop strong roots. It is purely in the mindset that someone who is giving everything they've got and actively participating in the team events, seeking out opportunities and knowledge will be easy to mentor and will blossom into wonderful leaders under your care.

27

Pulling Weeds

Your mind is a garden, your thoughts are the seeds.
It is your choice: you can grow flowers or you can grow weeds.
- William Wordsworth

Most gardens have their fair share of weeds, and yours will be no different. Weeds happen to good people. In your garden, these weeds will often manifest themselves in the form of frustration, anger, or jealousy. Your budding leaders are under stress from a new environment and business they are learning more about with each day. As common mishaps happen, perhaps a mistake with a sign up, a glitch with a member order, or any number of minor new business issues, new leaders can easily get frustrated. This is where you shine as a leader. It is your job to assist them and show them how expertly they will learn to manage these situations. Rarely, issues with other leaders in your garden, or even leaders from other team gardens, will bring about a disagreement or anger. Perhaps it was a perceived threat, an intentional one, or simply a misunderstanding. Whatever the case, as the gardener, it is your responsibility to help your budding leaders figure out how to resolve the situation with the least amount of dirt slinging throughout the gardens. Jealousy is perhaps one of the most wearisome challenges you may face as a gardener. We are all human and this emotion is simply part of human nature whether we want to acknowledge it exists or not. Perhaps one of your budding leaders is experiencing jealousy over your attention with another section of the garden, or concerning the rank and growth of one of the others. Whether your budding leaders are experiencing this deadly weed, or others around them have fallen victim, jealousy can get out of control if not handled immediately. We would all like to think our garden is a Nirvana of beauty, and these weeds would not dare enter, but the harsh reality is there. Weeds happen. Great gardeners keep peace in the garden without getting lost in the weeds.

28

Personality Conflict

*By plucking her petals you do not gather
the beauty of the flower.*

You will have leaders on your team whose personality just doesn't mesh with yours. As their leader and mentor, it is your job to support them anyway. No one said you have to be best friends with everyone on your team, but you do have to try your best with everyone on your team. Sometimes, rarely, but it does happen, your leaders will get a sense of entitlement. A feeling you owe them something. Perhaps they feel you are not doing enough, working hard enough, giving enough. Whatever the issue may be, please realize it is *their* issue. If you can honestly say you have given 100% (with the wisdom to know there will be days where you can give less and days where you give ever so much more) then you have done all that is in your power to do. Can some people run circles around you with their over-packed schedule and ability to handle many tasks with grace and ease? Yes. To some people, you will seem like that person. We all know someone we feel does ten times more than everyone else, and others who do ten times less. We are each gifted with certain talents and abilities and they are different for each person. We cannot compare ourselves to others. It is self-defeating. It is the comparison of apples and oranges. Why go there and make yourself feel less than you are, or make someone else seem so? You can choose to work through these perceived issues, or you can offer your support and continue on with the rest of your team. There will be people you will never satisfy or can never do enough for as a leader and friend. After repeated attempts, often it is best just to realize this personality conflict and let it be what it is: two great leaders with different visions and ideals on what virtues constitute a great leader.

29

The Myth of Multitasking

The dream is free, the journey is not.
-John Maxwell

There is a myth, started a long, long, long time ago, that people have the ability to multitask. You hear it all the time. You probably think you do it all the time. Why, just last week you were cooking dinner while talking to your friend on the phone, while answering your son's math homework questions, while helping your three-year old use cookie cutters at the table making play dough dinner, while setting the table, while baking dessert, while greeting your husband who just walked in the door. By the time dinner gets on the table, you aren't satisfied it is your best – after all, your rice is a little firm still and the veggies a little limp, the cobbler you had in the oven got a bit too toasty, your son looks more confused than ever with his math worksheet, the dishes are half set on the table, your three-year old has play dough in her hair and teeth, and you absentmindedly muttered "uh huh" "oh, really?" "oh yea?" "uh huh" at your friend's recounting of her latest adventure, all the while kissing your tired husband half-heartedly as he stepped through the door wanting to be greeted like the conquering hero. Well done. You "multitasked." Don't disillusion yourself with the ideal of multitasking. There is no such thing. You cannot do multiple things at the exact same time successfully. Once you embrace this fact, and start scheduling your tasks, you will find time for all of those things individually. Your dinner and dessert will taste great... possibly – if you are a great cook. Your son's homework and daughter's play dough will be keepsake worthy...maybe. You will really connect with your friend over her enthusiasm in sharing her adventures...definitely. You will greet your husband at the door and kiss him so thoroughly he will feel as if the mighty Zeus, himself, would be jealous. You will be in the *moment*. You will connect with your children, your husband, your tasks, even yourself, in a way you never have before when attempting the oft sought, never mastered, mythical "multitasking." *Live in the moment.*

30

The Spirit of the Garden

Growth takes time. Be patient.
And while you're waiting, pull a weed.
- Emilie Barnes

Happiness isn't always an easy emotion to cultivate. We strive to be happy and are often successful at achieving it. However, every now and again, whether the weeds are driving us crazy or something else has cast a rain cloud over our garden, we find it difficult to find our way through the mud and back into the sun. Do not fear. This is completely normal. If every moment were sunshine and happiness, we would lose all appreciation. It is the occasional rain cloud which makes us truly thankful for the sun. While you cannot fake happiness, nor should you try, you can be deliberate in your attitude. Your attitude will determine your success in the garden. Your leaders will respond to a great attitude. They will respond more vehemently to a poor attitude. Ever heard the saying: a positive story travels to a dozen people, and a negative story travels to a thousand people? Attitudes are much the same. Your positive attitude will affect all of those you encounter. You will build them up, champion their efforts, and celebrate their successes with a great attitude. If you get tangled in the weeds of issues and ugliness, your negative attitude will carry.

It won't just be the dozen or so people who witness this destructive attitude that are affected. News will travel through the garden faster than lightning strikes. Your team will avoid you, lose respect for you, and seriously wonder why they are part of your garden. Attitude can be the greatest nutrient in a garden, or the fastest poison. In all things – even those that disappoint you or frustrate you – keep a good attitude.

31

An Attitude Challenge

A dream without a goal is a wish.
- Larry Elder

There are a few things that can challenge the best attitude. One of the biggest challenges most budding business builders face is company sponsored incentive programs. What are these, you ask? Well, some of the most fun, challenging, and frustrating races you will ever participate in and conquer! Throughout the years, these incentive programs have changed, but the purpose has remained constant: help you grow the business of your dreams and reward you for your diligent efforts! Whether you are in a time race to gain rank, a "Drive to Win" race to grow teams and OGV, or some other company incentive program, you will be challenged to give it your all, help others grow their businesses, and do it all with unparalleled enthusiasm, effort, and speed. If you have set your team up for success by utilizing the Rising Star Team Bonus to structure your organization, you should have no problem with these challenges. Even if you do not have the RSTB structure in place, these are still great possibilities and worthy of the effort. Not to mention they are so much fun and really bring together a team like nothing else.

Truly, this team effort will yield great relationships, insight into how to grow your business stronger, and stretch and grow you in ways you never imagined. You know that saying about how it takes a whole village to raise a child? These races are much the same way. It takes a whole team to grow a leader to a certain rank. Your team will have fun helping you reach these goals – honestly, they are some of the best team bonding experiences if you let them be. Leaders who try to tackle these challenges alone will find frustration, exhaustion, and loneliness. Your team is your family. Let them be part of the fun and experience. They know when it is their turn, you will be all in and ready to shoot for the stars for them, too.

Ways to get your team to have fun and help your team grow:

- Offer your own personal challenge to leaders, such as attaining a certain OGV for a prize.

- Reward leaders who host classes or events.

- Offer sign up specials for membership and essential rewards.

- Be creative and think of something your team would love!

Incentive programs really are wonderful, but they don't come without a few risks. By now you are thinking, "Okay, here is where I find out something bad happens to me if I don't make the goal." Nope. Nothing happens. Unless you let it happen. You see, if at the end of the designated incentive month you don't capture Silver, Gold, Platinum, highest OGV, most sign ups, etc., you are still amazing. You have challenged yourself and grown. You also then have an unlimited time frame to get to the end goal. Would it really destroy you to make Gold in three years versus Gold in one? Would it crush you to get so close to winning the "grand prize" of a promotion and come up short? No. No, it would not. You will be a touch melancholy. We all find feeling sorry for ourselves an easy task. Then we realize we gave it our all and grew. We grew budding leaders, teams, and volume. We were successful at growing leaps and bounds. We should still rejoice! Sadly, though, sometimes a budding leader will take an unchecked goal as a failure. They view it as a shattered dream, losing heart and giving up entirely. Why? A prize for making rank or getting massive sign ups in a specific time was not the holy grail of all that is wonderful and perfect. It was just a mile marker along the way to Diamond. Who cares if you did not make this particular goal? You aren't shooting for Silver, Gold, or the most sign ups for a trip to Hawaii. You are shooting for Diamond. Keep your focus on the end goal. Being tied to time frames and countdowns can drive you insane. Coming upon the end of an incentive program lacking what it takes to get there leaves you feeling downtrodden and hopeless. Don't go there. You are too great of a leader to be worried about the incentive gift. Go for it. Go for it with all of your heart and soul, backed up by a team filled with excitement and expectations for success. If in the end, efforts weren't quite enough, know there is always a fun challenge around the bend and prepare your team to launch like a rocket into the next one!

32

Promotions

*The watering of a garden takes as much judgement
as the seasoning of a soup.*
- Helena Ely

You will see many leaders or teams offer promotions of their own, in addition to what Young Living also has monthly. Sometimes these promotions encourage membership, group growth, OGV growth, or attaining rank. Many times, these are just the push your team needs to accomplish a great goal. Great care must be taken when considering a promotion and its effects on your team. Numerous factors can impact whether or not your promotion is a smashing success or an abysmal failure.

When hosting classes, to encourage attendance, many leaders will offer a special sounding something like this, "Bring three friends with you and get a free bottle of grapefruit oil!" Why this works: everyone loves free stuff and no one likes to attend a class by themselves. We all want our buddies with us to have a fun social event away from the kids or responsibilities. Getting something free for doing something you want to do anyway sounds like a win/win situation! Where it can go wrong: offering something too valuable to encourage this promotion is subsequently capitalized upon, "Bring three friends and get a free bottle of Frankincense!" Yeah, right. So no one in their right mind is going to offer a promotion like this, but you see the issue. Quite often, the promotion simply breaks the bank and is not a realistic offering to stay within your business budget. Imagine, Maggie brings Sarah, Beth, and Jessica. She now gets a grapefruit oil costing you around $10. When those ladies sign up, they are going under Maggie as enroller and sponsor – remember, you did not know them, they are not your sign ups. Maggie is on your third level so you are making 4% commission on her personal volume. Now she has three new sign ups – *wonderful and amazing* – on whom you are receiving 4% commission. You would get a total of $12 commission on their sign up with a Premium Start Living Kit. The grapefruit you gave away to encourage these sign ups has paid for itself. So, imagine you gave away the bottle of Frankincense. At almost $80, you would need about twenty sign ups to accomplish the same goal and not be upside down in your promotion.

Another great promotion idea is to offer a travel case, oil, or diffuser pendant to encourage members to sign up for Essential Rewards. Sometimes this works beautifully: a level one member signs up and you get $8 back from their first 100pv autoship order. If your promotional gift was less than this, you have successfully paid for this promotion. If the cost was double this, in two months of 100pv Essential Rewards, you are still doing great. What if the person signing up for this promotion is on level five, and your rank is not high enough for you to get a generational commission on this level yet. You also offered a $20 gift as a promotion. How long will it take you to break even from this promotion? Now before you go and write off ever doing this promotion, think about this: eventually, you will be paid commission on this level, and even if they are deep within your levels and you only receive generational pay for the levels they are in, still, commissions will come. What then? Think about this: If you have leaders whose Essential Rewards you are helping firmly establish by your promotion, you are growing their OGV, which in turn, is helping your OGV. This will help you increase in leg volume, overall volume, and membership – directly affecting your rank and pay. Maybe budding leaders in your garden will make a new rank based on your incentive! Perhaps the $20 promotion now is worth the stability and windfall later?

Sometimes, promotions will be offered to one team in your organization and not another. Why? Why would you show preferential treatment to one budding leader and not another? For the simple reason that, just as in a garden, you would not give extra water to a plant already wet, but instead would give the water to the dry plant. Everything in a garden has a growing cycle and different nutrient and care needs. As a great leader, you *must* look to fill the needs of your budding leaders and growing teams. Sometimes this *does* mean a promotion for one team and not another. Once again, there is no room for jealous weeds in the garden. Encourage your leaders to view this, not with jealousy, but with wisdom so they learn from your example and grow forward, duplicating your actions within their own teams.

The larger your team grows, the harder it will be for you to offer group promotions. Try instead to offer raffle promotions or limited winner promotions. With a team of 10,000, offering a promotion where they receive a free oil or product for a certain personal volume will see you spending about $8,000 in products and mailing. Not to mention the time it takes to package all of the items and head to the post office. This is unrealistic for any leader to imagine undertaking, but we've all been there and done a promotion that was a bit more than we expected on both our time and pocketbook. Instead, look at a promotion such as this: "For every 300pv order placed from May 1-31, you will be entered with one raffle ticket for our Summer of Ningxia Raffle! With each additional 100pv order, you will receive an additional ticket. On June 1st, one lucky winner will be chosen to win a Four Pack of Ningxia Red every month this summer from June through August!" At the end of May, instead of mailing out several hundred packages of product to several hundred members, drop ship from Young Living a four pack of Ningxia Red on your Essential Rewards directly to the member once a month for all three months. Now you have earned free oil points, received reduced shipping, had someone else handle all the mailing, and are only responsible for remembering one person's gift instead of spreadsheets of several hundred people. Not only this, but you just spent less than $500 instead of closer to $8,000 and chances are, you were successful at pumping up your team and getting them excited to participate in this promotion.

Once again, it is up to you whether you offer promotions or none at all. Don't feel pressure because you see other teams or leaders doing so. One note on offering promotions: don't do them every month. It encourages people to have a handout mentality and wait for you to offer bigger and bigger things each month before they purchase. Then on the months you pull back and offer no promotion, they won't order or will only order a small amount, holding out for the next time you offer a great promotion. Quarterly promotions are a good schedule to keep if you plan on doing them, with the exception of classes. If you are fond of a product raffle, giveaway, or door prize to encourage attendance and see results every time, go for it!

33

Over-Flowing Wheelbarrow

*God has overwhelmed me with blessings,
and I am led to share them with others.*

- Allan Houston

At some point as a leader with a large organization, you will find yourself like a gardener with a wheelbarrow over-flowing on a daily basis. The chores are too numerous, the needs of the plants too great, the tasks so large, it just requires two people. Most especially when you realize it is affecting your family. This is the time you recognize the need for an assistant. Do yourself a favor and just plan for this stage.

How this looks will be different for everyone. Some leaders find they love the challenge of business, but need help at home with organization, cleaning, cooking, etc. Others find the largest benefit comes with someone assisting in childcare. A great rule to live by is find the number of hours you want to work/relax/adventure. Then break this down on a calendar as we have discussed. Next, hire out the things which don't fit this schedule, you don't have time for, are lacking the skills for, or quite simply, don't have the desire to do yourself. A small example of this is lawn care. All of us know how to mow a lawn. No desire? No time? Guess what? There is a teenager in your neighborhood just dying to make a little more money. If you find yourself with no time for home-cooked meals but can't stand the thought of eating out, look into hiring someone to cook or contracting meals through a catering service. The time you will save and be able to devote to either family or business will pay for itself in lifetime dividends in either fabulous residual income you built while not having to take time out to vacuum, cook, or do other chores, or in memories with your children – which are priceless.

34

Seasons of Life

Man was designed for accomplishment, engineered for success,
and endowed with the seeds of greatness.
- Zig Ziglar

I n all you have read here, you have seen the seasons of life for a Young Living leader. Just as the four seasons of life yield warm and cold periods, times of high activity or calm, and a changing of life in the garden, so do your seasons. There will be months where you are on fire, your task list is miles long, and you feel as if you are burning your candle at both ends. This high activity period is your spring. Your growth in the garden. You will see new buds creeping up out of nowhere, fresh branches developing on your oak tree, and hundreds of leaves and flowers beginning to bud everywhere you turn. This new life and strengthening root system in the garden is time consuming and filled with long days of cultivating and encouraging this new growth to take hold and flourish.

After a period of intense labor, in blows your summer like a warm breeze of calm. In the summer months, just as in the garden, people are enjoying what the garden has yielded. They are celebrating and taking time off from work – having some much needed fun with their families, enjoying the fruits of their labor. You will see your class participation dwindle. Do not be concerned. They are out making memories. Use this slow period to work on your leaders and yourself. Summer will be your time to nurture your leaders, connect with new members, and perhaps offer a leadership challenge or adventure to your team or a promotion to encourage existing members to try out the Essential Rewards program.

All too soon, summer will be over and in comes fall with another flourish of activity. For home-based businesses, fall is a time of high activity. Families all come rushing back from summer vacations and family get-togethers to jump into a hectic school/work schedule. Like anyone who hasn't seen their friends in awhile, they are anxious for classes, socialization, and connecting with the friends they haven't seen in a couple of months. While it may seem that autumn is a time in the garden where things are losing their luster, nothing could be further from the truth. With autumn comes a sense of preparedness. Just like the garden losing its leaves to prepare for winter, people are much the same. We know the time to start hibernating in our warm houses or heading out for brief but cold and snowy adventures is right around the corner. We want to make the most of what time we have left. Your classes will be full this season. This is a time of preparation for you, your leaders, and your members. This is a great season to catch up on all those care calls, which could not be made in the summer.

With the sounds of Christmas bells come the festivities and family activities, which will keep everyone busy until the New Year. In your business, you will see things slow down as people make time for family. Just as it should be. This doesn't mean you get to take the season off. Host autumn events during November and perhaps a cookie exchange with essential oil infused baked goods or a Christmas special to your members and leaders. Start preparing for the New Year. With January comes the rush of spring again.

Yes, just as in a garden, there really are no periods of rest. The seasons will come and go, both in nature and in your business. What you do with them is entirely up to you. A great gardener, just like a great leader, takes in the beauty of every season and evaluates the efforts required, determines the tasks needed, and gives their full attention to each undertaking. Every leader has a unique way of guiding and developing their team. Focus all your efforts on your garden of leaders and you will cultivate leaders as strong as oak trees, all with their own amazing gardens.

35

Final Thoughts

Wherever life plants you, bloom with grace.
– French proverb

Know this: if you put heart into everything you set out to do, give it your all, and lead with integrity and humility, you will not fail. Don't sweat the small stuff or minuscule details. Look at the big picture and focus on the long term. Some of your ideas will yield great rewards; others will need to be tweaked a bit before you see results. Your leaders will become your best friends and family. Serve them. Honor them. Celebrate them. *Love them.* In the end, as you sit in the shade of an oak tree in your very own Versailles, with your friends and family near, you will know success is not measured in money. True success is measured when you can look around your extensive gardens and see all the lives you have changed, all of the families you have helped, and how each of them have, in turn, blessed your life. Then, *and only then*, can you consider yourself successful.

Hopefully, as we come to the close of this book, you have learned a ton and gotten a few ideas along the way. In the end, it isn't about who put in the most money, time, or efforts. It is about who put in the most heart -- the most time in the relationships. They will shape and define both you and your garden.

Give everything you've got towards the relationships and the rest will naturally follow.

36

Garden Fertilizer

Even the greatest of creations began as small seeds.

The tips and ideas in this section are just that -- tips and ideas. You can use any and all of them or create your own! Some of these ideas may or may not work depending on the size of your team, the location of your garden, or the dynamics of your members. Read through them, garner a few ideas and plan, then go for it! These ideas are fun and encourage team spirit and relationship building. Make sure you allow your budding leaders to join you in hosting, planning, and implementing. Not only do they need the experience, they need to see and learn, firsthand, the work that goes into creating a phenomenal organization!

To encourage new sign ups, think about offering a sign up special, such as a product credit or perhaps an essential oil gift.

Get budding leaders to host classes by offering a challenge: a raffle ticket for each class hosted during the month – more classes, more chances to win. At the ending of the month, raffle off a fun prize like Ningxia Red, an Essential Oils Desk Reference, or perhaps items from the Young Living Gear website.

Recognize your team with small gifts when they make rank advancements or achieve a special goal!

Call three Young Living team members a week just to touch base and build your relationship. Don't make it all about business!

Look at your downline towards the end of the month. If you see Essential Rewards boxes without a check mark, this means their order did not process. They could have taken their grace month, but what if they didn't? An expired credit card could cause them to miss out on rewards! Call or message to check with them.

Make sure you check all of your business members have pv on their account for the month: 50pv for bonus money, 100pv to earn full commission. Find out quickly: green numbers mean they are above 100, orange means above 50 and red means NO COMMISSION!

Leadership Events and Retreats

Reward your budding leaders with a retreat filled with gardening tips and essential nutrients! A simple over night or weekend in a cabin or fun location will reset your energy and enthusiasm. Discuss leadership development, building strategies, and empower your team to grow their garden. While there, build dream boards highlighting all you want to accomplish in the next year. Make it better by bringing scrapbook supplies, magazines to cut up, and fun decorations to apply on dream boards. Encourage your team to put the dream board up at home where they can see it everyday!

Throughout the year, look for opportunities to celebrate your team. An elegant tea at a charming tea house, dinner out with the gang, a girls' night in, an adventure out and about – there are a lot of ways to show you care, recognize their hard work, and celebrate their efforts. These special gatherings will go a long way to cementing your friendship for a lifetime.

Membership Education and Promotions

Host an Ironman challenge during the slow summer months. Give budding leaders a series of business challenges worth various points, and watch them conquer new heights. Offer tiered prizes based on tasks completed.

Tips for Promotions

To increase OGV during slower gardening seasons, consider offering a member promotion, such as a free travel case, reference books, or diffuser pendant with purchase of 300pv. This will enable them to not only get all of Young Living's monthly specials, but a really neat gift from you as well.

Build your Essential Rewards membership by entering everyone who signs up during a two-month period into a raffle where one lucky member wins a new home diffuser!

A Year of Classes

Below are some suggestions for classes throughout the year. They are interesting, fun, and unique. They will inspire members to try new oils, join Essential Rewards, and truly love this company and their oils. This list is just to get you started and give you a few ideas. There are a ton of really great events and classes you can come up with on your own if you do a little brainstorming.

JANUARY

New Year, New YOU! Start the year of right with a Health Challenge. Host a class about weight management, aging gracefully, supporting muscles when exercising, and using Slique, Protein Power, Ningxia Red, Cool Azul, and Young Living supplements to maintain vibrant health. Make it better by challenging members to partake in a 60-day Ningxia Red challenge: They must order the Ningxia Red 8 Pack and drink 2-4oz a day for 60 days while eating healthy, maintaining a health journal daily, and trying their choice of other Young Living products. Provide members with research and information on Ningxia Red. Upon completion, anyone who participated and did the full challenge is rewarded with a bottle of Ningxia!

FEBRUARY

Host a Valentine's Make & Take, filled with love recipes. Body butters, lotions, bubble bath gel, and chocolate recipes all infused with essential oils are sure to make it a Valentine's Day no one will forget! Make it better by having organza draw string bags with a few wrapped chocolates to enclose gift jars.

Tips for Make and Take Events: Be sure to charge a nominal fee to cover your costs in these special classes. With make & takes, it is often best to do a flat fee regardless of what is made. Most leaders set the prices at $5 an item, or five for $20 so people are encouraged to try five new items. With other classes, it will depend on ingredients and supplies needed.

MARCH/APRIL

Make Easter memorable with a Healing Oils of the Bible Study. Hearing how essential oils were used in the times of Jesus will make this season one of the most poignant. Do you know Hyssop was the last thing Jesus smelled? Inspire members to delve deep into scripture with a beautiful class filled with friendship, faith, and love!

MAY

Join forces with other team members or crossline gardeners to host make & takes, vendor events, seminars, or other fabulous events. Inviting others for the adventure decreases your workload, increases camaraderie in the garden, and develops a team spirit. Not to mention, it is a blast!

JUNE

Host a Summer Survival Make and Take event all about camping, fishing, swimming, and playing in the summer months, while using Young Living to maintain health and wellness!

JULY

Grilling is all the rage in July! Host a Young Living cooking class where members learn about using essential oils to cook and grill with at home or camping this summer. Make it better by making a dish everyone can bring home for dinner. Keep it simple, no seven-course meals!

AUGUST

School is right around the corner! Highlight a back to school class for kids. Allow parents and kids to learn about being healthy throughout the year – everything from staying healthy with Young Living supplements and oils to making healthy snacks using essential oils. Make it better by hosting a play dough making station using essential oils to create fabulous healthy, great smelling dough.

SEPTEMBER

As we head into the fall months, we need to concentrate on keeping our skin and bodies hydrated. With lack of humidity, we all dry out and tend to age like the leaves falling from the trees. Host a Beauty Skincare class focusing on our largest organ: skin! Educate on how we can maintain health and wellness on the outside by what we put on the inside.

OCTOBER/NOVEMBER

These are great months to show your members the power of Ningxia. Host a class all about body systems and how they can support their efforts in health and wellness by using Ningxia Red. This has the added bonus of preparing your team to be knowledgeable and excited for January's upcoming Ningxia Challenge!

DECEMBER

We all get busy around Christmas. It can be difficult to keep the momentum going during the holidays. Consider hosting a Make & Take Holiday Open House where members come to make Young Living essential oil gifts to send off for Christmas. This is a great time to pass around the Christmas catalog and talk about all the great holiday products. Make it even better with a wrapping station and holiday treats!

Host a Cookie Exchange where everyone comes with their favorite cookie recipe made with Young Living essential oils. Trade cookies and recipe cards while sampling some delicious homemade cookies! Make it even better with some holiday drinks, like wassail, apple cider, or cocoa spiced with Young Living essential oils!

Other great classes:

Supplements	Men's Health	History of Oils
Going Green	Supporting Teens	The Art of Distillation
Heart Health	Hormone Health	Young Living
Brain Health	Business Building	Einkorn & Digestive Health
Sports Class	Green Cleaning	
Pregnancy & Babies	Emotional Health	Holy Oils of the Bible
Healthy Aging	Chemistry of Oils	

Recommended Garden Fertilizer

BOOKS:

On Business

Road to Royal, Debra Raybern

The Four Year Career, YL Edition, Richard Brooke

25 to Life, Adam Green

Circle of Success, Monique McLean

Driven, Jake Dempsey

The Young Living Lifestyle Book, Jordan Schrandt

How Big is Your Wave?, Teri Secrest

Do Over, Jon Acuff

Go Pro, Eric Worre

Oola, Dave Braun and Troy Amdahl

On Oils

Essential Oils Reference Guide, Life Science Publishing

Taming the Dragon Within, LeAnne Deardeuff

Inner Transformations..., LeAnne Deardeuff

Healing Oils of the Bible, Dr. David Stewart

The Chemical Free Home Series, Melissa Poepping

Chemistry of Essential Oils Made Simple, Dr. David Stewart

Releasing Emotional Patterns…, Carolyn L Mein D.C.

Nutrition 101, Debra Raybern, Sera Johnson, et al.

Gentle Babies, Debra Raybern

Homemade Mommy Beauty Essentials, Lindsey Gremont

Welcome Book, Jordan Schrandt

Essential Oils Integrated Medical Guide, D. Gary Young

Ningxia Wolfberry: The Ultimate Superfood, D. Gary Young

**Look for several other great books by D. Gary Young.

Websites:

Life Science Publishing – Essential oil resources & supplies

www.discoverlsp.com

Growing Healthy Homes – Essential oil resources & supplies

www.growinghealthyhomes.com

Crown Diamond Tools – Essential oil business supplies

www.crowndiamondtools.soundconcepts.com

Oily Boost – Essential oil logos, website, & graphics

www.oilyboost.com

B. Design - Branding, print, & websites

www.beebuzzworthy.com

Oily App – Mobile Young Living guide

www.oilyapp.com

You Infuse – Essential oil business resources & supplies

www.youinfuse.com

Oily Tools – Business tracking & management tools.

www.oilytools.com

Homemade Mommy – Info on essential oils & healthy living

www.homemademommy.net

Oil Revolution Designs - Graphics & Printables

www.oilrevolutiondesigns.com

Rank Duties

Star

- Open all of your oils and try them out!

- Sign up for Essential Rewards.

- Study one essential oil or supplement each week. Learn everything you can!

- Build a library of essential oil information.

- Print and read the Policies and Procedures of Young Living.

- Print and read the compensation plan.

- Start sharing your new passion with friends and family.

- Offer samples or information to interested people.

- Send a care package to new sign ups: books, supplies, welcome letter.

- Teach classes or meet individually to teach about Young Living.

- Attend Young Living's annual convention.

Senior Star

- Keep studying one essential oil or supplement each week.

- Add business related books to your library.

- Study the compensation plan. Know the basics of entire plan, concentrate on Star-Executive section.

- Create an online group or sharing page to reach far and

wide.

- Continue sharing with friends and family.

- Start meeting with new or potential leaders to share knowledge and ideas.

- Maintain contact with team: care calls/messages.

- Teach recurring member classes to broaden members' knowledge of oils.

- Recognize leaders in your team for making new ranks!

- Send out newsletter or monthly postcard with Young Living promotions.

- Attend Young Living's annual convention.

Executive

- Keep studying one essential oil or supplement each week.

- Keep adding more business and essential oil books to your library.

- Study the compensation plan. Concentrate on Silver-Platinum section.

- Post regularly in your online group or sharing page.

- Continue sharing with friends and family.

- Have recurring bi-weekly meetings with your leaders.

- Maintain contact with team: care calls/messages.

- Teach recurring member classes to broaden members' knowledge of oils.

- Recognize your team for making new ranks!

- Teach team leaders how to support their team and do all

tasks for their rank.

- Begin participating in vendor events or bazaars.
- Broaden reach by advertising locally and online.
- Help support your team leaders' promotions and events.
- Send out newsletter or monthly postcard with Young Living promotions.
- Attend Young Living's annual convention.

Silver

- Keep studying one essential oil or supplement each week.
- Keep adding more business and essential oil books to your library.
- Concentrate on Silver-Platinum compensation plan section.
- Post regularly in your online group or sharing page.
- Continue sharing with friends and family.
- Have recurring bi-weekly meetings with your leaders.
- Maintain contact with team: care calls/messages.
- Teach recurring member classes to broaden members' knowledge of oils.
- Recognize your team for making new ranks!
- Teach team leaders how to support their team and do all tasks for their rank.
- Participate in vendor events or bazaars.
- Broaden reach by advertising locally and online.
- Help support your team leaders' promotions and events.

- Send out newsletter or monthly postcard with Young Living promotions.

- Attend Young Living's annual convention.

- Attend retreats you have qualified for throughout the year.

Gold

- Keep studying one essential oil or supplement each week.

- Keep adding more business and essential oil books to your library.

- Concentrate on Silver-Platinum compensation plan section.

- Post regularly in your online group or sharing page.

- Continue sharing with friends and family.

- Have recurring bi-weekly meetings with your leaders.

- Maintain contact with team: care calls/messages.

- Teach recurring member classes to broaden members' knowledge of oils.

- Recognize your team for making new ranks!

- Step back and watch Silver and below leaders to take the lead for their teams.

- Participate in vendor events or bazaars.

- Broaden reach by advertising locally and online.

- Send out newsletter or monthly postcard with Young Living promotions to lines without a Silver leader. Encourage Silver leaders to do the same.

- Host a retreat or event for your team leaders.

- Join other crossline leaders to host essential oil events.

- Attend Young Living's annual convention.

- Attend retreats you have qualified for throughout the year.

Platinum

- Keep studying one essential oil or supplement each week.

- Keep adding more business and essential oil books to your library.

- Concentrate on Diamond-Royal Crown Diamond compensation plan.

- Post regularly in your online group or sharing page.

- Continue sharing with friends and family.

- Have recurring bi-weekly meetings with your leaders.

- Maintain contact with team: care calls/messages.

- Teach recurring member classes to broaden members' knowledge of oils.

- Recognize your team for making new ranks!

- Encourage Silver and below leaders to take the lead for their teams.

- Participate in vendor events or bazaars.

- Broaden reach by advertising locally and online.

- Send out newsletter or monthly postcard with Young Living promotions to lines without a Silver leader. Encourage Silver leaders to do the same.

- Host a retreat or event for your team leaders.

- Join other crossline leaders to host essential oil events.

- Attend Young Living's annual convention and retreats you have qualified for throughout the year.

Diamond-Royal Crown Diamond

- Keep studying one essential oil or supplement each week.
- Keep adding more business and essential oil books to your library.
- Concentrate on Diamond-Royal Crown Diamond compensation plan.
- Post regularly in your online group or sharing page.
- Continue sharing with friends and family.
- Have recurring bi-weekly meetings with your leaders.
- Maintain contact with team: care calls/messages.
- Teach recurring member classes to broaden members' knowledge of oils.
- Recognize your team for making new ranks!
- Encourage Silver and below leaders to take the lead for their teams.
- Participate in vendor events or bazaars.
- Broaden reach by advertising locally and online.
- Send out newsletter or monthly postcard with Young Living promotions to lines without a Silver leader. Encourage Silver leaders to do the same.
- Host a retreat or event for your team leaders.
- Join other Young Living leaders to host essential oil events.
- Attend Young Living's annual convention and retreats you have qualified for throughout the year.
- Consider speaking at events for Young Living and other leaders.

Amanda Uribe

Bibliography

Dellinger, S. (1989). Psycho-geometrics: How to use geometric psychology to influence people. Prentice Hall Direct.